Notes on
Instrumentation and Control

Notes on Instrumentation and Control

G. J. Roy, CEng, FIMarE, MRINA

Foreword by
W. D. Ewart, CEng, FIMarE, MRINA

NEWNES

Newnes
An imprint of Butterworth-Heinemann Ltd
Linacre House, Jordan Hill, Oxford OX2 8DP

A member of the Reed Elsevier plc group

OXFORD LONDON BOSTON
MUNICH NEW DELHI SINGAPORE SYDNEY
TOKYO TORONTO WELLINGTON

First published by Stanford Maritime Ltd 1978
Reprinted 1981
Revised and reprinted 1983
Reprinted 1987
Reprinted by Butterworth-Heinemann Ltd 1994
Reprinted 1995

ISBN 0 7506 1837 X

Printed and bound in Great Britain

Contents

Contents

Foreword

Written by experienced lecturers at one of Britain's leading marine engineering colleges, each book of this series is concerned with a subject in the syllabus for the examination for the Second Class Certificate of Competency. It is intended that the books should supplement the standard text books by providing engineers, where appropriate, with numerous worked examples as well as easily understood descriptions of equipment and methods of operation. In the first six books extensive use is made of the question and answer technique and throughout the Series specially selected illustrations enable the reader to understand and remember important machinery details.

While the books form an important basis for pre-examination study they may also be used for revision purposes by engineers studying for the First Class Certificate of Competency.

Long experience in the operation of correspondence courses has ensured that the authors treat their subjects in a concise and simple manner suitable for individual study—an important feature for engineers studying at sea.

W. D. Ewart

Preface

This book provides basic information on the instrumentation, control engineering theory, control equipment and control systems employed in marine applications.

Although aimed at the requirements of the Second Class Certificate of Competency Examination for Marine Engineer Officers, the text has been extended in many cases to provide a deeper penetration into the theory and problems involved in operating control equipment on board ship in the hope of reducing the effect of mis-informed adjustments. It is also intended to provide useful revision for those Engineer Officers preparing for their First Class Certificate.

The diagrams are not necessarily drawn to scale and in general show the type of simplified sketch required for examination purposes. The Candidate should attempt to do as much as possible of the sketch freehand as time does not permit the extensive use of drawing aids in the examination.

G. J. Roy

Acknowledgements

The author wishes to thank the following firms and institutions for their assistance, both with information and diagrams:
The British Ship Research Association
The Institute of Marine Engineers
Bailey Meters and Controls
Foxboro-Yoxall
Negretti & Zambra Ltd
Fisher Governor Co Ltd

SI UNITS

Mass = kilogramme (kg)
Force = newton (N)
Length = metre (m)
Pressure = newton/sq metre (N/m^2)
Temperature = degrees celcius (°C)

CONVERSIONS

1 inch = $25 \cdot 4$ mm = $0 \cdot 025$ m
1 foot = $0 \cdot 3048$ m
1 square foot = $0 \cdot 093$ m^2
1 cubic foot = $0 \cdot 028$ m^3
1 pound mass (lb) = $0 \cdot 453$ kg
1 UK ton (mass) = 1016 kg
1 short ton (mass) = 907 kg
1 tonne mass = 1000 kg
1 pound force (lbf) = $4 \cdot 45$N
1 ton force (tonf) = $9 \cdot 96$ kN
1 kg = $9 \cdot 81$ N
$0 \cdot 001$ in = $0 \cdot 025$ mm
$(°F–32) x\frac{5}{9} = °C$
1 lbf/in^2 = $6895 N/m^2$ = $6 \cdot 895$ kN/m^2
1 kg/cm^2 = 1 kp/cm^2 = 102 kN/m^2
1 atmosphere = $14 \cdot 7$ lbf/in^2 = $101 \cdot 35$ kN/m^2 = 760 mm Hg
1 bar = $14 \cdot 5$ lbf/in^2 = 100 kN/m^2

Note: For approximate conversion of pressure units

100 kN/m^2 = 1 bar = 1 kg/cm^2 = 1 atmos
1 $tonf/in^2$ = 15440 kN/m^2 = $15 \cdot 44$ MN/m^2
1 HP = $0 \cdot 746$ kW.

CHAPTER 1

Pressure Measuring Devices

MEASUREMENT OF PRESSURE

Two basic types of instrument may be used to measure absolute pressure, gauge pressure, draught or vacuum pressure and differential pressure (Fig. 1). One is the liquid column, in which the density and liquid height are used to measure pressure, the other the metallic formed elastic type such as the Bourdon tube, diaphragm or bellows, using in some cases an opposing spring. A modification of this second form is a non-metallic type for measuring very low pressure, which invariably incorporates a spring.

Fig. 1

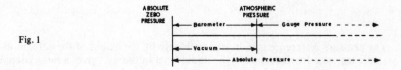

LIQUID COLUMN (U-TUBE MANOMETERS) (Fig. 2)

Liquid placed in connecting legs of a U-shaped tube will indicate the difference in the pressure acting on the top of the two legs. The height of the displaced liquid gives a direct indication of this pressure difference. $P_2 - P_1 = d \times h$ where P_1 and P_2 are the pressures on the two sides of the column, d is the density of the manometer liquid and h is the difference in height of the columns.

Depending upon the application one limb may be open to atmospheric pressure and the 'h' indicates the 'gauge' pressure or the pressure relative to atmospheric pressure.

This would be the case with a water filled manometer used for low pressures,

Fig. 2   Manometer

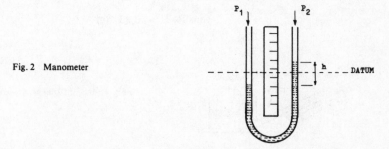

such as checking combustion air pressures for a boiler, with a range of about 0–100 mm. When filled with mercury, higher pressures can be measured and a similar device could be used for checking scavenge or turbo-charger air pressures. With the two limbs connected across, for example, the inlet and outlet trunkings of a charge air cooler, the difference in height indicates the pressure drop across the cooler and gives an indication of the degree of fouling of the tubes. The manometer is a simple, reliable and accurate device and is found in many modified forms to suit particular applications. To allow easier readings to be taken, the scale may be enlarged by making one leg into a well as in Fig. 3.

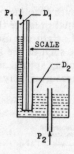

Fig. 3   Well Type Manometer

The pressure difference is indicated now only by the height of the column in the single leg, as a small change in the liquid level in the well gives a large change in the column level. Provided the ratio of the diameter is very large, errors due to a change in the liquid level in the well can be ignored.

$$P_2 - P_1 = d \left(1 + \frac{D_1}{D_2}\right)h$$

D_2 diameter of well
D_1 = diameter of leg

As long as $\frac{D_1}{D_2}$ is small compared to unity, when this term is ignored the error is negligible and $P_2 - P_1 = dh$

Fig. 4 shows a further modification which enables small pressure differences to be read more accurately, and is known as an 'inclined tube manometer'. By having the small diameter limb at an angle, the length of the scale is increased for a given head.

$$h = L \sin A$$
$$\text{thus } P_2 - P_1 = d \times L \sin A$$

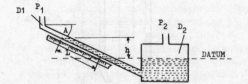

Fig. 4   Inclined Tube Manometer

For the water manometer 1 m³ of fresh water has a mass of 1 Mg (Mega-gram or 1 x 10⁶ grams) and weighs 9·81 x 10³ Newtons. Thus 1 mm of fresh water produces a pressure of 9·81 Newtons/m². The relative density of mercury is 13·6 and hence 1 mm of mercury produces a pressure of 9·81 x 13·6 Newtons/m² or 134 Newtons/m². (0·134 kN/m²). Manometers may be used as a permanent fixed instrument, but dirt can affect their efficiency and they are susceptible to physical damage. They may be used as portable devices for periodic checking of pressures or for checking other pressure measuring instruments, but they are very sensitive to position and must be accurately levelled before use.

The mercury barometer is an application of the well type manometer comprising basically a glass capilliary tube, sealed at one end and approximately 900 mm long, filled with mercury and then inverted into a container of mercury open to atmospheric pressure. (See Fig. 5)

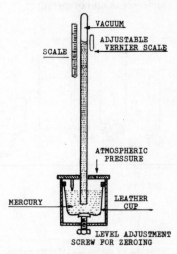

Fig. 5 Barometer

The space above the mercury in the capilliary tube is now under vacuum conditions (a Torricellian vacuum—where any pressure present is due to the vapour pressure of the liquid), and a column of mercury rises up the tube, balanced by the atmospheric pressure acting on the surface of the mercury in the reservoir. Altitude and temperature will affect the readings but the former is of course not applicable to marine uses.

Normal atmospheric pressure supports a column of mercury 760 mm high and thus atmospheric pressure = 760 x 0·134 = 102 kN/m² = 1·02 x 10⁵N/m² = 1·02 Bar.

Variations in the climate can affect the atmospheric pressure and these can be reflected in gauge readings when true absolute pressures are required. This is particularly so in steam turbine plant operation where condenser back pressure is of importance to plant efficiency. A drop in atmsopheric pressure due to a change in climatic conditions can cause an apparent loss of vacuum or increase in back pressure. If, for example, with the barometer at 760 mm of mercury the normal optimum condenser gauge reading is 725 mm of vacuum, then the back pressure is equivalent to 35 mm of mercury. If due to a change in climatic

3

condition the barometer drops to 735 mm, and the gauge reading drops to 700 mm, there is an apparent rise in the back pressure equivalent to 60 mm of mercury until the barometer reading is taken into consideration; then it can be seen that the 25 mm change in atmospheric pressure is reflected in the gauge reading change and the condenser back pressure is still equivalent to 735–700 = 35 mm. To provide an accurate reading of condenser pressure a *Kenotometer* is used, which is basically a manometer subject to condenser pressure. The tube A, Fig. 6, is evacuated and sealed at the top so that it is filled with mercury when the condenser is under vacuum condition, the pressure drops on the surface of the mercury in reservoir B and a Torricellian vacuum is drawn in the closed tube A. When a high vacuum is reached in the condenser the scale is adjusted until the zero mark coincides with the mercury level in B and the small column of mercury supported by the incomplete vacuum is measured as the absolute pressure in the condenser in mm of mercury.

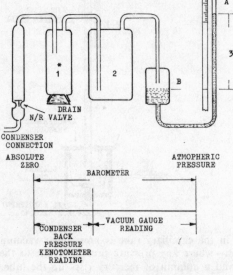

Fig. 6   Kenotometer

1. MOISTURE TRAP
2. CALCIUM CHLORIDE MOISTURE ABSORBENT
3. HEAD OF MERCURY SUPPORTED BY BACK PRESSURE ABOVE ZERO IN CONDENSER

ELASTIC TYPE GAUGES

This type of gauge depends basically upon Hooke's Law for its operation in that within the elastic limit stress is proportional to strain and deflection is thus proportional to the pressure applied. There are three types of gauge in this class, bourdon tube, bellows and diaphragm.

The bourdon tube is probably the most common of all the types of pressure gauge in use, mainly due to its simplicity and versatility. Behind the basic simplicity, however, is a behaviour under pressure whose analysis is extremely complicated and suffice to say that this type of gauge consists basically of a tube of oval cross section shaped in a circular arc over approximately 270°. One end of the tube is fitted into a block for connection to the vessel or pipe line whose internal pressure is to be measured whilst the free end is sealed and connected to a suitable linkage or a sector and pinion gear design. As the pressure inside the tube is increased, the tube tends to change shape from oval to circular cross section and in doing so causes the tube to straighten thus moving the free end. The free end movement is only about 5 mm and the linkage is required to give sufficient magnification for accurate indication of the pressure to which the tube is subjected. Over the designed operating range the pointer movement is approximately linear in relation to the applied pressure.

The tube may be made from a variety of materials including phosphor bronze (copper 95 per cent, tin 5 per cent + trace of phosphorus) for pressures in the range 1·03 Bar to 70 Bar; beryllium copper (98 per cent copper, 1·8 per cent beryllium, 0·3 per cent cobalt) for pressures in the range 0·3 Bar to 350 Bar; and stainless steel (16 per cent chromium, 10 per cent nickel, 2 per cent molybdenum) for pressures in the range of 2·0 Bar to 70 Bar, where there is a requirement for corrosion resistance. Where there is no such requirement, one of the first two materials would be used. The thickness of the tube wall depends upon the range of measurements required and the dimensions of the tube should be sufficient to produce a force rendering the effects of frictional force negligible. The linkages and quadrants etc. may be of brass or phosphor bronze, but bakelite quadrants carried by bakelite plates have been found to withstand rough treatment somewhat better than these materials. Vibration is the major cause of damage to and malfunctioning of all types of instrumentation and every effort should be made to avoid subjecting instruments and control equipment to situations where vibration is a problem. Even if the mounting is vibration free, machinery such as high speed or reciprocating pumps can cause vibrations so creating excessive wear on gauge linkages and gears and work hardening the tube. Closing in the gauge shut off cock may help and small shock absorbing spring loaded dampers may be fitted, whilst filling the case with glycerine could be beneficial in damping out vibration.

With bourdon tubes the normal working pressure should not be more than 60 per cent of the maximum range so that inaccuracies due to changes in the tube material from fatigue are unlikely to arise. Should the gauge be overloaded to the extent that the pointer goes off the scale, a permanent set may occur in the tube, whilst the link gear could be deformed, the quadrant and pinion come out of mesh and then re-engage in a new position so that the pointer is no longer in its correct relationship to the tube position. A typical bourdon tube arrangement is shown in Fig. 7.

To increase accuracy and response by reducing friction and inertia and lost motion the tube may be wound into the form of a spiral, as shown in Fig. 8 similar to a watch spring. As the movement increases in proportion to the distance along the arc of the tube increased free end movement can be obtained. This makes it extremely convenient for use in instrument cases, such as recording pressure gauges, where space is limited. The useful range here is about −1·0 Bar to 15 Bar.

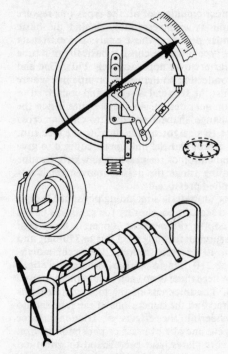

Fig. 7   Bourdon Tube Gauge

Fig. 8   Spiral Tube Type

Fig. 9   Helical Tube Type

A greater deflection of the element for a given pressure change has been obtained for higher pressures requiring tubes of increased wall thickness by winding the tube in the form of a helical spring, Fig. 9, and eliminating the necessity for any form of amplifying mechanism, such as a segment and pinion, and the friction and lost motion which that entails. A 1:1 ratio, between spring movement and pen travel, can be achieved with a pen travel of $45\frac{1}{2}°$. This can be used for pressures up to 400 Bar. Gauges are usually calibrated at 20°C and large variations in ambient temperatures can affect accuracy, sensitivity and life. Any gauge used on steam or hot vapours should be fitted with an efficient syphon tube or pipe loop, filled with condensate to keep the tube from direct contact with the hot medium.

Many ships are now fitted with equipment for testing pressure gauges, usually in the form of a deadweight tester as shown in Fig. 10. The system is balanced at atmospheric pressure by opening the reservoir valve and moving the piston so

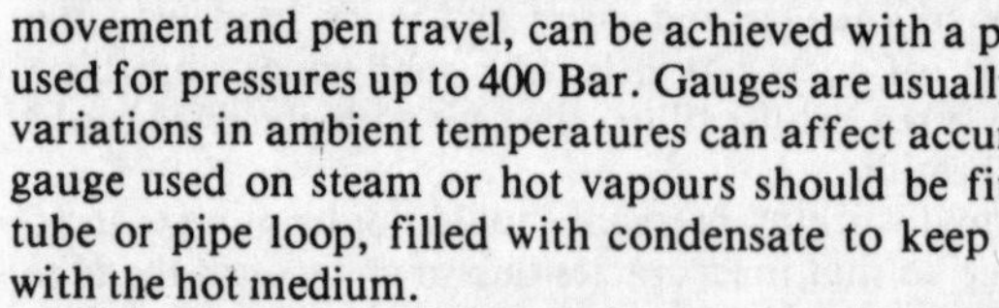

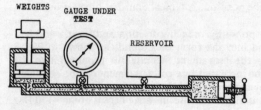

WEIGHTS

GAUGE UNDER
TEST

RESERVOIR

Fig. 10 Gauge Testing Equipment

that the cylinder is full of oil. The floating piston then takes up its lowest position. The reservoir valve is closed, and the handwheel operated to raise the pressure. The increase in pressure on the underside of the floating piston and the load thus produced is balanced by the load due to piston weight, weight carrier and calibration weight. When equilibrium is reached the gauge under test will record the pressure in the chamber. To reduce friction on the piston, it should be spun slowly.

Another method is to use a very high equality precision gauge in place of the piston and weights as a comparison. By varying the pressure over the required range the accuracy of the gauge under test can be compared with the precision gauge. To check a gauge a definite procedure should be adopted, first to check the gauge and then to adjust it. If the gauge is corroded, badly damaged or obsolete, it should be scrapped. To check a gauge, place it in the test rig and test for leakage by raising the pressure to about 25 per cent above the scale maximum and hold for 10 secs. Release the pressure slowly to zero, when the pointer should follow. If it fails to do so and does not return to zero even after tapping lightly, then the tube is in poor condition and the gauge should be replaced. If the pointer does return to zero, raise the pressure again to the gauge maximum and release slowly, watching for jerky movement or a tendency to stick. This indicates wear, leakage or a damaged hair spring. Following a satisfactory check so far, raise the pressure in a series of steps and then drop it in similar steps, noting any errors that occur. If these errors are less than $1 \cdot 0$ per cent and the hysteresis does not exceed $0 \cdot 25$ per cent, then the gauge is worthy of recalibration. After cleaning, subject the gauge to a pressure of about 15 per cent in excess of the dial reading and then select two points at about 10 per cent and 90 per cent of the dial range as test points. The magnification and reading at the former are checked and modified by adjusting the slides in the quadrant slot, Fig. 11 and by removing and resetting the pointer respectively until the gauge gives the correct reading at both points. The mid-point reading is then checked by adjusting the length of the connecting link between the quadrant and tube. After tightening all screws, the gauge is finally checked at all points on the scale.

Fig. 11 Gauge Adjusting Mechanism

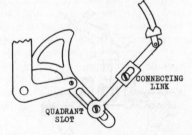

CONNECTING LINK

QUADRANT SLOT

Hysteresis is a term used to provide a true overall picture of an instrument under varying conditions. It is achieved by increasing the pressure in a series of steps to a maximum and then repeating at the same points when the pressure drops from the maximum to zero. If these points are plotted on a graph, the resultant curve gives the error at each point and the hysteresis of the instrument.

The accuracy of an instrument may be defined as the closeness the instrument reading approaches to the true value, whilst the sensitivity may be defined as the ratio of output to input or the least signal input that can create an output signal having the required characteristics.

A modification of the bourdon tube gauge, shown in Fig. 12, is the *diaphragm sealed gauge*, used where a general purpose gauge is not suitable owing to corrosion or plugging etc. Here a diaphragm is fixed between two flanges to seal the line fluid from the gauge, and the tube is filled with a suitable liquid to transmit the pressure from the diaphragm movement to the bourdon tube. For highly viscous fluids which solidify in stagnant ends, the use of a diaphragm seal type gauge is recommended. In some cases purging may be necessary. Where fluids to be measured are non-compatible with the gauge or diaphragm materials, the diaphragm and gauge body may be coated with rubber or P.V.C. This reduces accuracy and a hysteresis of 2 per cent of the scale reading may arise. Bellows and diaphragm type gauges have their particular applications, the former being used in control equipment for measuring pressures due to their compactness and robustness whilst diaphragms types are generally found in the lower pressure ranges.

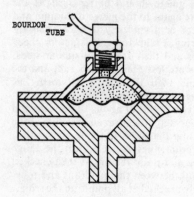

BOURDON TUBE

Fig. 12 Diaphragm Sealed Gauge

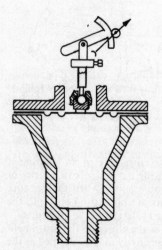

Fig. 13 Schaffer Gauge

The *Schaffer diaphragm-spring-type* pressure gauge can be used in place of the sealed pressure bourdon tube type gauge described above, where a cheaper gauge is required, see Fig. 13. This type of gauge can also give a better and more positive indication than the bourdon tube type of gauge for low pressure work. The deflection of a diaphragm shell is determined by the diameter, metal thickness, corrugation shape, modules of elasticity, pressure applied and the number of corrugations. Normally they are designed to give a linear relationship to the pressure applied over as wide a range as possible with reasonable sensitivity, but by decreasing the corrugation depth and number, sensitivity is increased and linearity reduced. In some designs two metal diaphragms are joined together at their peripheries to form a capsule, as shown in Fig. 14. The diaphragms are pressed or punched out with a central hole and then welded or soldered together to form a stack. Brass, phosphor bronze, beryllium copper or stainless steel may be used, and their diameter is not usually more than 100 mm. Pressure measurements are normally in the range 25 mm to 3500 mm water gauge. Some designs incorporating a single large diaphragm may be used for draught measurement as in combustion control systems. Such diaphragms may be of phosphor bronze or non-metallic material such as Teflon or Neoprene, the movement of the diaphragm being opposed by a spring. These are sometimes known as *slack diaphragm* gauges, see Fig. 15.

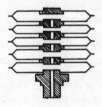

Fig. 14 Capsule Stack

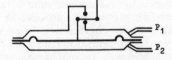

Fig. 15 Slack Diaphragm Type Gauge

The bellows type gauge is a development of the diaphragm capsule type, being formed in one continuous process from a thin seamless tube into a deeply folded or corrugated unit either mechanically or hydraulically. Materials are usually brass, stainless steel, phosphor bronze, monel and beryllium copper, the type of material depending upon whether corrosive conditions are present.

To ensure as long a life as possible a bellows movement is generally restricted by an opposing spring so that only a small percentage of the maximum stroke is used. This type of device can be used for pressure measurement over a wide range, including absolute pressure and differential pressure gauges.

The measurement of the difference between two pressures, or differential pressure measurement, usually achieved by a *D.P. Cell*, is used extensively in instrumentation and control engineering as a means of detecting changes in the flow of liquids or gases, changes in liquid levels or merely to detect a difference in pressure between two points in a system. The 'U' tube manometer can be used

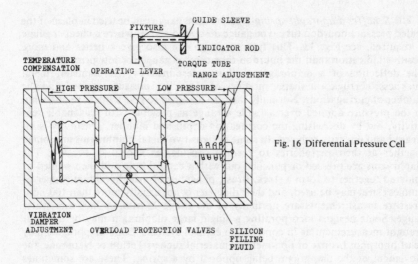

Fig. 16 Differential Pressure Cell

for such work as explained previously and Fig. 16 shows an application of a bellows differential gauge pressure cell which could be used to indicate the pressure drop across a lubricating oil filter and producing an alarm if the pressure drop exceeds a given value. Testing would be carried out approximately monthly by shutting the downstream connection to the main pipe line and opening the drain, which must return to a save-all or drains tank. The space inside and between the two bellows is filled with a silicon based fluid with a constant viscosity over a wide temperature range. The effect of the higher-pressure is to compress the left hand bellows and force the fluid into the right hand bellows, expanding these. The spindle movement is opposed by the reference spring loading and the resultant movement is converted into pointer movement by the torque tube arrangement. To prevent damage due to overloading, protection is provided by the valve which shuts the interconnecting passage between the bellows. Some such devices have an adjustable orifice between the two bellows to reduce the effect of rapid fluctuation in flow.

Fig. 17 shows an *aneroid barometer* which could be considered an application of the diaphragm type gauge. This consists of a thin cylinder with the upper surface corrugated, the space inside being evacuated so that the pressure of the atmosphere tends to collapse it. As atmospheric pressure increases the centre of the corrugated area moves down, taking the tensioning spring with it and thus moving the bell crank. This then slackens the chain or wire operating the pointer spindle and the return spring on this takes up the slack and in doing so moves the

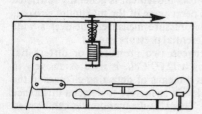

Fig. 17 Aneroid Barometer

pointer. A drop in atmospheric pressure allows the tensioning spring to lift the diaphragm centre, re-adjusting the bell crank so that it moves the pointer spindle against the return spring. The diaphragm may be made of phosphor-bronze or cupro-nickle, the remainder of the components being of brass or steel.

CHAPTER 2

Temperature Measuring Devices

LIQUID IN GLASS THERMOMETER

Probably the most common liquid for this type of thermometer is mercury. The volumetric expansion of mercury is about 8 times that of glass and thus when heated in a glass container mercury will occupy an increased volume. This change of volume forces the mercury up the capilliary tube attached to the bulb and the height of this column is then used to indicate the temperature of the liquid or gas surrounding the bulb by means of a suitable scale. For moderate temperatures in the range $-38°C$ (freezing point of mercury) to $350°C$ the space above the mercury is vacated. To extend the range up to $600°C$ a quartz mercury thermometer is used and the space above the mercury is filled with nitrogen or CO_2 under pressure to suppress the boiling point of the mercury ($360°C$). For low temperature measurement, pentane is used for temperatures in the range $-196°C$ to approximately $100°C$ and alcohol or tuolol in the range $-80°C$ to approximately $100°C$. There are two types of mercury in glass thermometers; the total immersion type, where the thermometer is immersed up to the reading and the partial immersion type where the thermometer is immersed to a specified depth. The former is the more accurate.

BI-METALLIC STRIP THERMOMETER (Fig. 18)

These thermometers depend for their operation upon the fact that different metals have different coefficients of thermal expansion, and by brazing together two metals, one with a high coefficient such as copper, and the other a low thermal coefficient, such as INVAR (36 per cent Nickel, 64 per cent Fe) a bi-metal strip is formed. When heated the unequal expansion of the two materials rigidly fixed together causes the strip to deflect. The degree of deflection is a function of the temperature change and by forming the strip into a helical coil and connecting this to a mechanical linkage at one end and fixing the other, the coil can be made to wind and unwind as the temperature varies and move a pointer across a temperature scale. Range is approximately $-40°C$ to $320°C$

FILLED SYSTEM THERMOMETERS

There are three versions of this type of thermometer which can be used for remote temperature indication and/or operation of alarm or control circuits. All involve the use of a bulb at the sensing end, and a capilliary tube connecting the bulb to either a bourdon tube, bellows or similar device which responds to change in pressure due to a variation in volume.

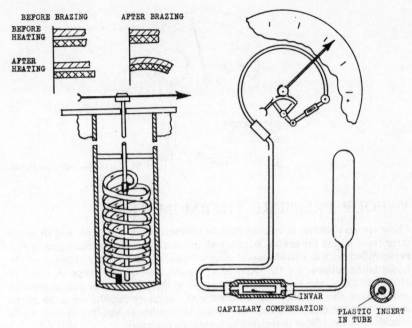

Fig. 18 Bi-metal Strip Thermometer   Fig. 19 Mercury in Steel Thermometer

LIQUID FILLED THERMOMETERS (Fig. 19)

A typical liquid filled or liquid expansion type thermometer consists of a bourdon tube connected to a metal bulb by a small bore metal tube known as a capilliary tube, the whole internal volume of the bulb and tubes being filled with liquid with a high coefficient of cubical expansion. The system is completely sealed and to avoid any problems with vapour pressure effects or a difference in head between the bulb position and the gauge, the system is pressurized to about 70 Bar in the mercury filled type. In operation any variation in the temperature being measured varies the volume of the mercury and it is this volume change which operates the bourdon tube, pressure changes being incidental. The instrument has a linear relationship with temperature change, the range of operation being approximately –39°C to 520°C for mercury, and the power sufficient to operate a pointer as pen for a recorder or a pneumatic transducer. If the capillary tube, which is about 0·2 mm in diameter, or the bourdon tube are subjected to temperatures appreciably different from those at which calibration was carried out, errors in the measurements obtained may arise. If the ratio of the volume of the capilliary to bulb can be kept large enough the effect is small and for distances below 15 metres the fineness of the capilliary tube does not produce any appreciable errors. Above this figure, to keep the bulb small and thus response good, compensation may be provided by the means shown in Figs. 19 and 20. Another means of compensation can also be provided by means of a bimetallic strip between the tube tip and the quadrant linkage.

13

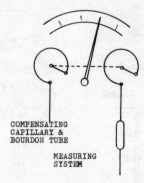

COMPENSATING
CAPILLARY &
BOURDON TUBE

MEASURING
SYSTEM

Fig. 20 Temperature Compensation

VAPOUR PRESSURE THERMOMETERS

These are very similar in construction to the mercury in steel type, and there are three types within the group, but they all involve a completely evacuated system partly filled with a volatile liquid such as alcohol, the vapour pressure of the liquid being suitable for the required operating temperature range. A range of $-10°C$ to $300°C$ can be accommodated and as there is no error due to ambient temperature change, they can be used with capilliary lengths up to about 60 metres without compensation. The scale is non-linear and the system has a considerable time delay in registering temperature change.

GAS FILLED THERMOMETER

Again these contain the same basic elements as the two previous types, the system this time being evacuated and filled with nitrogen or helium under high pressure. If the mass and volume of the gas are considered constant, then the absolute pressure in the system is proportional to the temperature, so that a change in temperature at the bulb is shown as a change in pressure at the bourdon tube. The deflection of the tube is proportional to pressure and hence to the temperature, giving a linear relationship. Ambient temperature changes can produce errors and compensation is limited to a bimetal strip at the bourdon tube tip. They are most useful when the capilliary tube length can be limited to about 2 m so that runs through varying temperature areas are limited and connected via a bellows to the operating mechanism of a pneumatic or electrical temperature transmitter. Range is about $-193°C$ to $600°C$. Problems have arisen with the gas permeating through the welds and bulb.

RESISTANCE THERMOMETER (Fig. 21)

Temperature measurement here is based on the temperature coefficient of resistance of a wire element which is wound as a helical coil around a hollow ceramic or mica former and then covered with a thin protective film. Operation depends upon the fact that when a metallic conductor is subject to a temperature change, the electrical resistance varies according to the law:

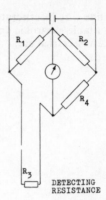

Fig. 21 Resistance Thermometer Bulb

DETECTING
RESISTANCE

Fig. 22 Resistance Thermometer Circuit (basic)

$$R_T = R_0(1 + \alpha T)$$

where R_T = Resistance at T°C. R_0 = resistance at 0°C
T = temperature change in °C and α = temperature coefficient for the
particular metal.

The wire used for the resistance may be of copper, platinum or nickel, the last
two in a high purity form being the most common, with platinum being most
favoured, despite high cost, due to its high resistivity. The windings are double
wound to eliminate the inductive effect. Wires are of about 0·02 mm to 0·8 mm
diameter.

Measurement is usually carried out by some form of Wheatstone Bridge
circuit with either a galvanometer or an electric potentiometer as a detector. In
the basic two wire system shown in Fig. 22, four equal resistances are coupled
together in the form of a Wheatstone Bridge and a current is applied to the
bridge by a battery. A galvanometer connected as shown will not deflect while
the resistance of the two parallel paths is equal. However if the temperature of
the air or gas surrounding one of the resistances changes, causing the resistance
wire temperature also to alter then the resistance of the wire will change according to the previous formula. This will upset the balance of the bridge,
causing a current to flow through the galvanometer the strength of which is a
function of the temperature change of the external resistance. In this two wire
system any change in the ambient temperature of the leads connecting the
distance resistance to the bridge will also affect the resistance on that side of the
bridge and produce an error. In most systems therefore a three wire type is used
with both sides of the bridge connected to the distant resistance so that any
change in ambient temperature affects both sides equally. For high accuracy a
four wire system would be used.

Also for high accuracy and to allow for automatic monitoring the balanced
bridge form of measurement is used as shown in Fig. 23. Here a centre zero
galvanometer is used so that by adjusting the slide wire contact A the bridge can
be balanced as the galvanometer is brought to zero (null balance) showing that in
the balanced condition there is no current flow in the galvanometer circuit. The

15

slide wire incorporates a scale reading directly in temperature units. By using a suitable electronic amplifier and reversible electric motor, automatic balancing can be carried out.

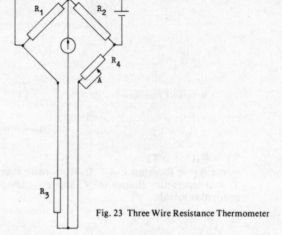

Fig. 23 Three Wire Resistance Thermometer

The resistance element would have a resistance of about 100 ohms at 0°C and the range is normally limited to about −200°C to +600°C although by using tungsten or molybdenum for example in specialized conditions temperatures up to 1200°C can be measured. Problems associated with the operation of resistance thermometers include the effect of vibration and strain on the wire, and keeping the current flow as low as possible commensurate with good sensitivity so that internal heating does not affect the accuracy of the resistance bulb. For a 100 ohm element the resistance of the leads is usually limited to about 3 ohms.

THERMOCOUPLES

If a circuit is formed consisting of two dissimilar metallic conductors A and B and the junctions are kept at different temperatures a current will flow in the circuit owing to two different e.m.f.'s being generated at the junctions. Fig. 24

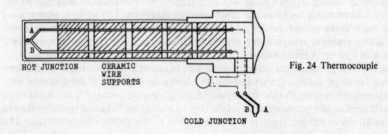

HOT JUNCTION   CERAMIC
                WIRE
                SUPPORTS

COLD JUNCTION

Fig. 24 Thermocouple

shows a simple thermocouple arrangement consisting of two dissimilar metal wire conductors with the two ends joined. Good electrical and thermal contact is essential for efficient operation. If the temperature of one end is raised whilst the other is kept at a fixed lower temperature and a sensitive meter is placed in the circuit an e.m.f. proportional to the temperature difference between the two ends is set up. As the e.m.f. generated is a function of temperature difference between the hot and cold junctions, allowance has to be made for any temperature variation at the cold junction. The instrument displaying the temperature is a very sensitive millivolt meter requiring only a small current for full scale deflection. For distant remote indication it would be feasible to leave the cold junction at the thermocouple head and extend the instrument wiring to the required read-out position. As the thermocouple output is only in the region of 100 millivolts, distant reading would need a degree of amplification and also any temperature variation at the head would effect the cold junction making the temperature reading inaccurate. This problem is overcome by extending the thermocouple wires by cables having matching properties so that the cold junction can be placed in a position where the ambient temperature is reasonably stable and adjustments can be easily made should the ambient temperature change. Frequently the cold junction is placed in the instrument case which may be in an air conditioned control room providing fairly stable conditions. Automatic adjustment of the electrical circuit to compensate for a temperature variation at the cold junction can be provided, one method being to attach a bimetal strip between a control spring on the instrument pointer end of the instrument case, so that any temperature change at the case will re-adjust the pointer. A Wheatstone Bridge circuit may also be used and where a number of thermocouples are in use, the cold junctions are brought adjacent to one another and kept at a constant temperature by a heater.

Thermocouples can be used over a range of temperatures from -250°C to +650°C and are commonly found in exhaust gas temperature measurement. They can be cheaper than resistance thermometers, do not require a stable reference voltage, can be made very small, and tend to stand up to vibration better than most resistance thermometers. However, the latter do not require cold junction compensation and have a high degree of linearity.

Besides the materials quoted in the diagram, other combinations include iron (+) constantan (-), chromel (+) [90 per cent nickel, 10 per cent chromium], alumel (-) an alloy with 94 per cent nickel, 2 per cent aluminium, plus silicon and manganese. These are known as Base Metal Thermocouples and have upper temperature limits of 850°C and 1100°C respectively. For higher temperatures, up to 1400°C, Rare Metal Thermocouples would be used such as an alloy of 90 per cent platinum, 10 per cent rhodium (+), and platinum (-). The leads connecting the thermocouple head to the instrument must have thermo-electric properties to match those of the thermocouple itself and in the case of the Base Metal instruments they would be of the same material, but for the Rare Metal type where long runs and large diameter cables are used to reduce resistance, electrical cost prohibits these metals being used as compensation cables and copper (+) and copper, nickel (-) would be used. It is essential that when connecting up the wiring, the correct wires are joined together otherwise other thermoelectric junctions will be formed.

THERMISTORS

A thermistor is an electrical device made of solid semi-conductor materials, which include metal oxides and their mixtures such as cobalt, copper, manganese, nickel and tin. Oxides in powder form are pressed into the desired shape which may include beads, discs or rods of varying sizes, to suit the particular applications. A bead could be $0 \cdot 4$ mm in diameter, a rod $0 \cdot 7$ mm to 6 mm in diameter and 50 mm long, and at the same time heat treated to recrystallize them, forming a dense ceramic body. Electrical contact is made by plating on the contacts, baking on metal ceramic coatings or embedding the wires before firing. The thermistor is then used in a similar manner to a resistance thermometer, but its operation differs in that with the thermistor, as the temperature rises, the resistance falls, i.e. it has a negative temperature coefficient of resistance, and the effect is much greater than the increase in resistance that occurs as temperature rises with the resistance thermometer. Thus, for a given temperature change a much larger working signal is produced by the thermistor. Being resistance devices they require a reference voltage for evaluation and would be connected into a Wheatstone Bridge circuit. Thermistors, being strong and rugged, are particularly suitable for bearing and stern tube temperature measurement and are used for temperature monitoring throughout some diesel engine applications. As the resistance curve shows, thermistors are particularly sensitive at low temperatures (Fig. 25).

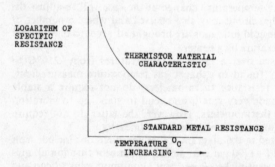

Fig. 25 Thermistor Resistance/Temperature Relationship

The use of the terms pyrometer and thermometer have been the cause of some confusion and a loose definition used frequently in the past for a pyrometer covered any type of thermometer capable of measuring relatively high temperatures. The tendence in recent times has been to regard all devices measuring temperature, which are in direct contact with the body, fluid or gas as thermometers, and devices which are not in direct contact as pyrometers. Some diesel engine manufacturers still refer to exhaust gas thermocouples as pyrometers, probably in deference to another definition which regards 500°C as the dividing line.

Fig. 26 shows the basic layout of a non-contacting pyrometer, one of a group known as radiation pyrometers. This is an optical or disappearing filament pryometer. Operation depends upon extreme sensitivity of the human eye to differences in brightness between two adjacent surfaces of the same colour. The

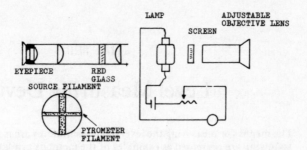

Fig. 26 Optical Pyrometer

radiation given off by a burner flame, for example, is measured by comparison with a source providing standard condition of brightness such as a tungsten lamp filament. By varying the brightness of the lamp so that it just disappears into the brightness of the burner flame viewed through the lens, the temperature of the flame can be measured from the meter reading, with modification for any filters used.

CHAPTER 3

Level Measuring Devices

The means for measuring the level of fluids in tanks are many and varied and the following are presented as examples of the methods available.

Gauge Glasses. The most direct method for indicating tank contents but susceptible to damage. These are usually only used for low and moderate pressures with the exception of the plate type and reflex glasses used for high pressures on boilers. It is not advisable to use gauge glasses on tanks containing inflammable fluids, but heat resistant glasses are available and these must be well protected from damage and have shut off cocks at top and bottom.

Float Gauges. Simple types for local indication employ a hollow cylinder, ball or sealed polystyrene disc floating on the surface of the fluid with a wire passing out through the top of the tank, over a pulley with a balance weight and indicator on the free end. The weight can also operate high and low level alarm contacts and a variable resistance may be incorporated to provide level indication.

An increasingly common application for a float operated device is the *magnetic float switch*, used for high and low alarm levels in boilers, storage tanks and bilge wells. A typical device is shown in Fig. 27. Another float type local reading gauge is shown in Fig. 28. Here the float, incorporating a magnet in contact with the tank liquid, moves up and down a profiled guide tube. A follower magnet moves in a sealed, evacuated glass tube to indicate contents.

Displacement Gauges. These operate on the principle that a body placed in a liquid is buoyed up by a force equal to the weight of the displaced liquid, The displacer must be part submerged in the fluid and as the fluid rises and falls and moves up and down the displacer, so the apparent change in weight that occurs is used to operate an indicator for the level. One method is to use a torque tube consisting of a tube, sealed at one end and open at the other, and with a flange welded to this end and fixed to the indicating instrument case. A rod is passed down the tube and welded to the sealed end. The free end of the rod extends into the instrument case and operates a pointer or a pneumatic or electrical transducer. The displacer arm is welded to the sealed end of the tube making an angle of 90° with this. As the liquid level varies so the apparent change of weight is balanced by the spring constant of the torque tube as it twists and thus moves the indicator rod. Any change in relative density of the liquid involved has to be compensated for. (Fig. 29)

Hydrostatic Type. A simple short distance remote reading type is shown in Fig. 30 where the gauge tube is filled with inert gas or air under pressure. As the liquid level rises or falls, the force due to the varying head of liquid on the diaphragm changes and alters the pressure of the air or gas in the tube, operating the bourdon tube gauge. Alarm micro-switches could be operated by the gauge pointer.

Bubbler System. Fig. 31 shows a simple bubbler system suitable for nearly all liquids, corrosive and those containing suspended solids.

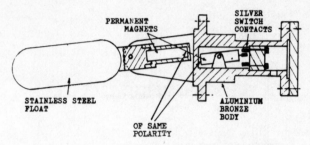

Fig. 27 Magnetic Float Switch

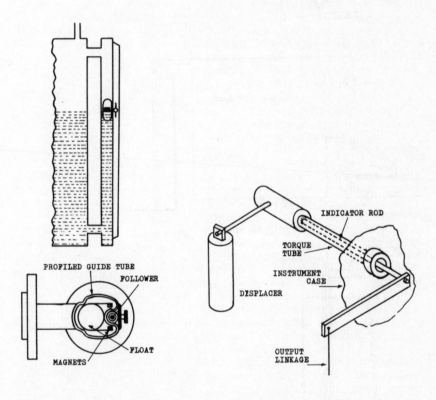

Fig. 28 Magnetic Float Gauge

Fig. 29 Displacer and Torque Tube Gauge

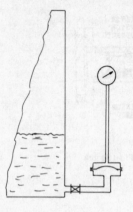

Fig. 30 Hydrostatic Gauge

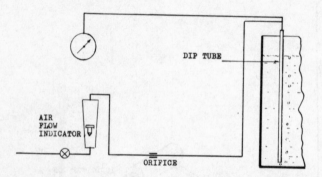

DIP TUBE

AIR
FLOW
INDICATOR

ORIFICE

Fig. 31 Bubbler Type Gauge

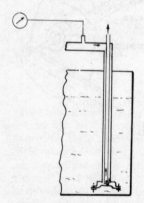

Fig. 32 Diaphragm Bubbler Gauge

Air under pressure is supplied via a flow indicator such as a Rotameter and an orifice—the latter to limit the air pressure in the dip tube so that when the tank is empty there is no pressure in the tube to give a false reading. The tube extends to about 75 mm above the sludge level line. As the liquid level rises, so the force exerted by the head of oil on the air pressure in the tube increases and this is used to operate indicators, alarms and control circuits. Indication is given of the actual weight of liquid; level will depend upon temperature and relative density.

Fig. 32 shows a modification suitable for liquids where gas or air bubbling through could create problems. It would be suitable for a lubricating oil drains tank contents indicator where the open type with air bubbling through the oil could cause oxidization trouble. The varying head of oil acts on the diaphragm and varies the flow of air from the tube and hence alters the air back pressure in the tube. This pressure then acts as a signal for indication, alarm and control purposes.

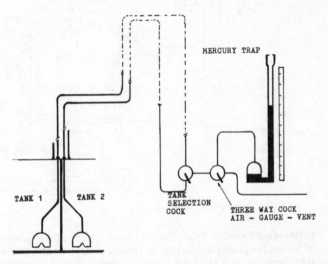

Fig. 33 Pneumercator Gauge

Pneumercator Gauge. Fig. 33 shows the layout of a typical pneumercator gauge commonly used for measuring the quantities of liquids in deep and double bottom tanks. It is basically a well type mercury manometer in which air is used to transmit the force exerted by the head of liquid in the tank to the manometer well. A hemispherical bell is placed towards the bottom of the tank above the sludge line, the bell having a V notch cut in it to give a datum level. Copper piping is run from the top of the bell via a well protected pipe run up to the top of the engine room or into the uptake space and then down to the control room, oiling station or a convenient (usually hot) engine room location. The loop high into the engine room is to prevent tank contents passing back into the gauge should tank over-pressure occur. The gauge has a trap to prevent the mercury being blown out should a blockage in the system arise. One gauge can be used to measure the contents of a number of tanks, frequently a pair of identical port and starb'd tanks, and a selector cock is provided to connect the gauge to the particular tank whose contents are to be measured. When this has been done the multi-way cock is turned to connect the pump to the system and isolate the gauge and the circuit is charged with air, usually about 10–15 strokes of the hand pump (excessive pumping does no harm to the system but exhausts the operator). The cock is then turned to connect the gauge to the tank, the head of fluid in the tank exerts a force on the air and the pressure is transmitted back to the well moving the mercury up the gauge tube so indicating the weight of oil in the tank. Level will depend upon relative density and temperature. Gauges may be calibrated for a fluid of a particular relative density or have an adjustable scale to accommodate a small range of relative densities.

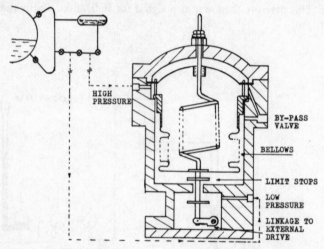

Fig. 34 Differential Pressure Cell

Differential Pressure Type. Fig. 34 shows the basic arrangement used in this type of gauge, frequently employed for remote indication of boiler water level and for supplying a signal for level control systems. For this instrument tappings are made on the steam and water sides of the boiler shell and fitted with shut off valves. The steam side is connected to a small condenser containing a weir so that a constant head of water is applied to one side of a d.p. cell. The water side is connected to the other side of the d.p. cell so that the variable water level is balanced against a constant head. Variation in level operates the cell, which produces a pneumatic or electrical signal. In this particular arrangement a bellows type has been used—the output spindle could operate a nozzle flapper device for a pneumatic signal on electrical transducer. To prevent an excessive pressure difference occurring over the cell, should one of the valves be shut, a balance leg is often fitted.

The Igema Gauge is a well known remote reading boiler water level indicator. Again it is basically a manometer with connections to the steam and water spaces of a boiler as shown in Fig. 35. The steam connection has a small condenser fitted with a weir which provides a constant head on this side of the tube. The

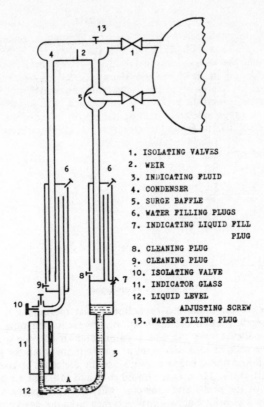

1. ISOLATING VALVES
2. WEIR
3. INDICATING FLUID
4. CONDENSER
5. SURGE BAFFLE
6. WATER FILLING PLUGS
7. INDICATING LIQUID FILL
                    PLUG
8. CLEANING PLUG
9. CLEANING PLUG
10. ISOLATING VALVE
11. INDICATOR GLASS
12. LIQUID LEVEL
                ADJUSTING SCREW
13. WATER FILLING PLUG

Fig. 35 Distant Reading Level Gauge

other leg is subject to the varying level of water in the boiler. For equilibrium the forces acting on either side of point A must be equal, thus in the left hand leg the constant head of water up to the condenser plus the coloured Igema indicating fluid head must equal the head due to the Igema fluid and the water in the right hand leg. As the level of water in the boiler rises, the head of the right hand leg increases and forces some of the Igema fluid from the reservoir into the left hand leg increasing the height of the fluid in the gauge. This movement also places some of the water from the weir which flows back to the boiler. The Igema fluid is non-mixable with water and has a higher relative density.

Electrical Capacitance Gauge. Fig. 36 shows the basic arrangement for such a gauge. A capacitor is a device for storing electrical charges and consists of two metallic plates placed close to one-another, but not touching, in an electrical circuit. If, with all other conditions kept constant, the air in the space between the plates is displaced by another substance it will be found that the value of electrical charges that the plates can store will vary. The substance between the plates is known as the dielectric and its ability to affect the electrical charge storage capacity or capacitance of the plates, is known as the dielectric constant or relative permittivity. (Air has relative permittivity of approx. 1; rubber 2 to 3·5). In the liquid level measurement application, a probe is inserted into the

25

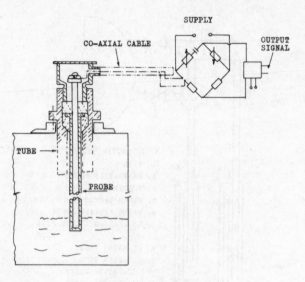

Fig. 36 Capacitance Level Gauge

tank and represents one plate of a capacitor, whilst the tank side or an open ended tube, depending upon the application, represents the other plate. The capacitance will be least when the tank is empty and air fills the space between the probe and the tube or tank side, and at a maximum when the air has been displaced by the liquid and the tank is full, since the dielectric constant of liquid is higher than that of air. Thus, as the liquid rises and falls, the electrical charge storage capacity of the probe and tube etc., will vary. The probe and tube are connected into an a.c. bridge network, which measures the degree of change in capacitance and hence level and produces a signal representing this. The a.c. bridge is supplied with a high frequency, low voltage current. The instrument can be used for measuring changes in level, as a high and/or low level detector and for detecting an oil/water interface in an oil/water separator.

The probe may be of stainless steel to combat any corrosion problems and if the tank liquid is a conductor of electricity, the probe would be sheathed in a non-conducting material, probably PTFE. The main drawback in using these gauges is the error produced should scum or a film of dirt form on the surface of the liquid and adhere to the probe. In their favour, they are simple, rugged, have high corrosion resistance, no moving parts, and are relatively low in maintenance requirements apart from cleaning.

The length of cable from the probe to the instrument is of major importance and the sheathed outer casing should not be interfered with as it forms part of the circuit.

CHAPTER 4

Flow Measuring Devices

Differential Pressure Type. As the name implies this type of flow meter utilizes a change in pressure of the fluid across a pressure reducing device placed in the pipeline to measure the quantity of fluid flowing. An orifice plate, flow nozzle or venturi may be employed to create the pressure drop, using the basic theory that energy can be neither created nor destroyed but transformed from one type into another. Assuming the unit mass and total energy of the fluid in the pipeline to be constant, then the kinetic energy plus potential energy immediately upstream of the venturi, which is the name given to this particular form of pressure reducing device, must equal that at the throat and:

$$\frac{V_1^2}{2} + \frac{P_1}{\rho} = \frac{V_2^2}{2} + \frac{P_2}{\rho} \quad \text{Where } \rho \text{ is the density of the fluid}$$

$$\text{or} \quad \frac{V_2^2 - V_1^2}{2} = \frac{P_1 - P_2}{\rho}$$

From this it can be seen that the increase in velocity of the fluid at the throat is a function of the square root of the drop in pressure between the entrance and throat, and the relationship follows the curve shown in Fig. 37.

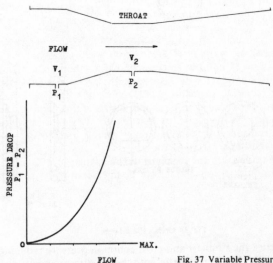

Fig. 37 Variable Pressure Flow Meter

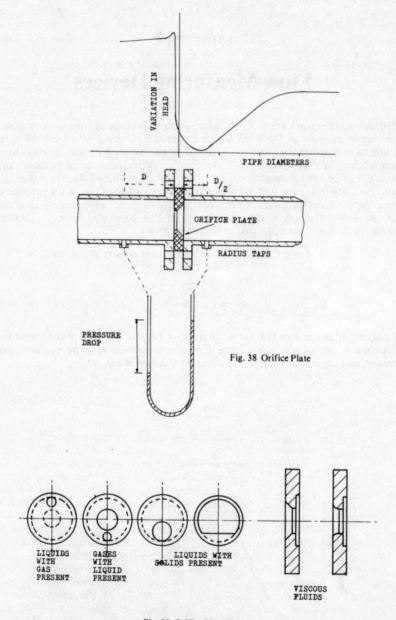

VARIATION IN HEAD

PIPE DIAMETERS

D

D/2

ORIFICE PLATE

RADIUS TAPS

PRESSURE DROP

Fig. 38 Orifice Plate

LIQUIDS WITH GAS PRESENT

GASES WITH LIQUID PRESENT

LIQUIDS WITH SOLIDS PRESENT

VISCOUS FLUIDS

Fig. 39 Orifice Plate Types

In marine practice the simplest and most common pressure reducing device is the *orifice plate*, (Fig. 38). It is inserted into the pipeline as shown, the diameter of the hole through the plate being sized to produce the appropriate differential pressure at the maximum rate of flow. The bore of the hole should have a square edge on the upstream face, with no burrs, and the plate should be perfectly flat and polished on this face. The hole must be concentric with the bore of the pipe and every precaution taken to see that the flow of fluid to and from the plate is smooth. There are varying figures quoted, but in general there should be at least 12 pipe diameters of straight pipe upstream of the plate and about 5 downstream, with no bends, partly open valves, and thermometer pockets or joints intruding into the piping, to ensure smooth flow. Fig. 39 shows the various types of orifice plate used for viscous fluids and fluids with a high solids content. To ensure the plate is placed the correct way round a tab giving direction is welded on the periphery.

When the flow of water passes through the orifice it continues to contract after passing the plate before commencing to expand. The plane of the minimum cross-sectional area, and thus the maximum velocity, is known as the *vena-contracta*. It is located approximately half a pipe diameter downstream of the orifice plate but its position depends upon the ratio of the orifice area to pipe area, (cross-sectional respectively) where the upstream pressure is measured, and could be up to $0 \cdot 8$.

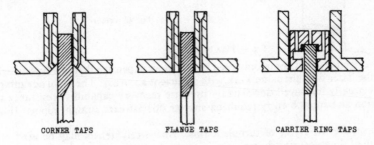

CORNER TAPS   FLANGE TAPS   CARRIER RING TAPS

Fig. 40 Pressure Tapping Arrangements

To measure the pressure drop across the orifice, tapping points for connecting the measuring devices have to be made. Any one of four standard positions may be chosen depending upon design and requirements, three as in Fig 40 and Fig. 38 and for best results the pressure tappings should be taken where the pressure gradients and turbulence are least. This could be one pipe diameter upstream and at the vena contracta downstream, but this theoretical advantage is minimal and it is common to place the downstream tap at $0 \cdot 5$ times pipe diameter downstream. They have the advantage of being areas where there is little turbulence and where welded bosses are not required they can be drilled and tapped into the pipe (making sure there are no burrs) and the connections screwed in flush to the interior of the pipe surface. Pipes can also be easily sprung apart for plate installation. *Corner taps* are used where the pipe diameter is not large enough to permit $0 \cdot 5$x pipe diameter tappings downstream. *Flange taps* may also be used for this purpose, but *carrier ring taps* come under this heading also. The latter have the added advantage of being accurately positioned by the manufacturer and not influenced by variations in pipe diameter, being in a machined component. Orifice plates for general use may be made of austenitic stainless steel, with monel metal for steam services as an alternative. For sea water monel metal may again be used, or alternatively, rigid nylon. Orifice plates are susceptible to distortion, scoring and erosion on the upstream face and sharp edge, which can cause a fall off in accuracy.

The *flow nozzle* shown in Fig. 41, has the advantage of requiring a shorter length of straight pipe upstream to give smoother entry than the orifice plate. It is less susceptible to errosion and will permit accurate measurement of approximately two-thirds more fluid at the same differential head than the thin plate orifice, and this is one of the main reasons for its choice. It also has a slightly improved pressure recovery and a discharge coefficient of 0·99.

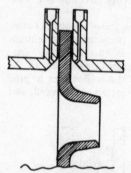

Fig. 42 Venturi

Fig. 41 Flow Nozzle

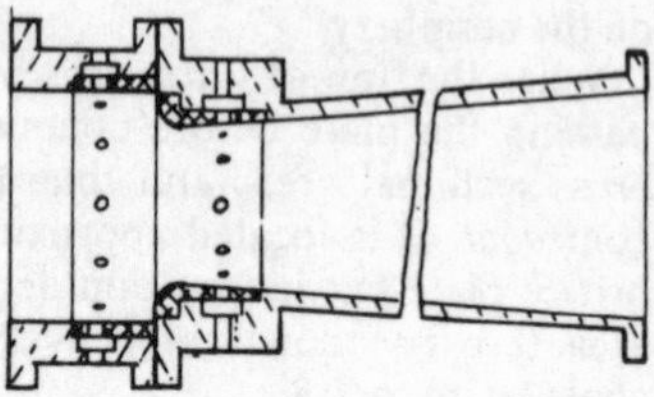

The *venturi* is not commonly used as it is more expensive than the flow nozzle and the latter does the same work with sufficient accuracy. The main advantage is the greatly improved downstream pressure recovery capability, resistance to errosion and smooth entry requiring shorter downstream straight piping. (Fig. 42)

To reduce the effect of turbulent flow, flow straighteners may be used upstream of the measuring device.

Square Root Extractor. Flow meters are usually used to provide a signal for process control purposes, and therefore, the differential pressure created is fed to a d.p. cell, where a pneumatic or electrical signal is produced for transmission into the control circuit. Because the flow/pressure drop relationship is not linear, except for very small flow variations where the non-linearity can be ignored, means have to be adopted to modify the signal so that it matches the linear signals of the remainder of the control circuit. This is achieved by a square root extractor as shown in Fig. 43.

Any change in flow in the pipe line causes a variation in the pressure drop across the orifice which is picked up by the d.p. cell bellows and thus a pneumatic transmitter is operated to produce a non-linear output signal related to the fluid flow change. This signal is then fed to bellows A. Assume it to increase, thus expanding the bellows and pivoting the force arm on diaphragm B towards the nozzle. Air flow from the nozzle is restricted and the buildup in back pressure operates the direct acting relay to increase the pressure on bellows C making angle α greater. The increase in pressure on diaphragm B and the force arm causes this to pivot about the pivot point, thus moving the force arm away from the nozzle. Equilibrium is thus restored to give a linear output signal which is the square root of the input signal.

The triangle shows the relationship of the forces, with R the longitudinal

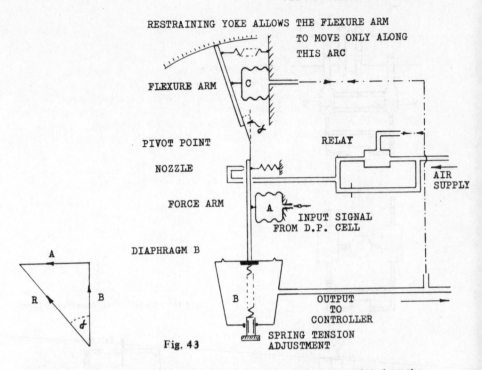

RESTRAINING YOKE ALLOWS THE FLEXURE ARM
TO MOVE ONLY ALONG
THIS ARC

FLEXURE ARM

PIVOT POINT

NOZZLE

FORCE ARM

DIAPHRAGM B

RELAY

AIR
SUPPLY

INPUT SIGNAL
FROM D.P. CELL

OUTPUT
TO
CONTROLLER

SPRING TENSION
ADJUSTMENT

Fig. 43

restraining force on the flexure arm. Force A is directly proportional to the input pressure on bellows A. Force B is directly proportional to the output pressure. Tan α = A ÷ B or B Tan α = A. Angle α is only allowed a 0–6° variation, and as for small angles the tangent of the angle varies directly with the angle, the expression can be written B α = A. As the position of the flexure arm creating angle α is directly proportional to the pressure in the bellows C, and this bellows is also connected to B, then B can be substituted for α and thus B^2 = A or B = $\sqrt{A}$ (i.e. output pressure is the square root of the input pressure to give a linear signal representing change in fluid flow).

In general an overall error of 1 per cent of the maximum scale reading occurs with d.p. instruments.

VISCOUS FLUID FLOW

For fluids such as heavy fuel oil which require heating to give them a sufficiently low viscosity for pumping and which could coagulate in small dead end pipe lines to d.p. cells and gauges, seal pots containing a suitable low viscosity non-mixable fluid such as ethyl-glycol (anti-freeze) are used as in Fig. 44.

VARIABLE AREA FLOW METERS

Fig. 45(a) shows one type known as a Rotameter. Here the float rises and falls in proportion to the rate of fluid flow through the tapered tube, thus adjusting the annular area between the float and the tube wall. Equilibrium is achieved when the downward gravitational force on the float is balanced by the upward force

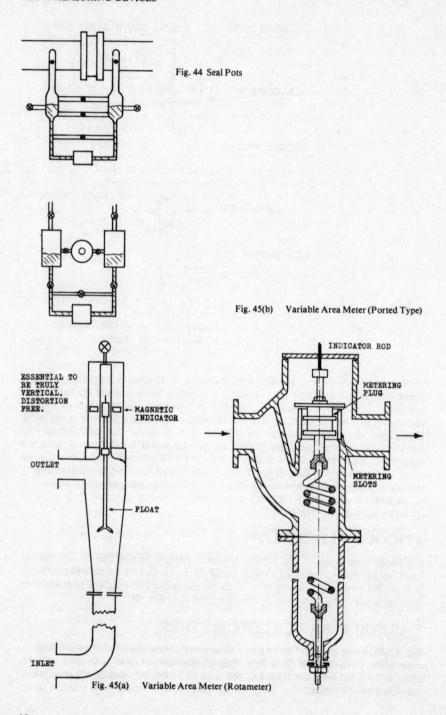

Fig. 44 Seal Pots

Fig. 45(b)   Variable Area Meter (Ported Type)

ESSENTIAL TO
BE TRULY
VERTICAL.
DISTORTION
FREE.

INDICATOR ROD

METERING
PLUG

MAGNETIC
INDICATOR

OUTLET

METERING
SLOTS

FLOAT

INLET

Fig. 45(a)   Variable Area Meter (Rotameter)

32

exerted by the fluid. This depends upon the flow rate and annular area, and the position of the float thus adjusts itself to any change in flow so that its height is proportional to the quantity of fluid flowing. The tapered tube may be of glass for local indication, except where hazardous fluids such as oil or chemicals are being measured or where extremes of cold are likely to be met. A magnetic indicator can then be used. Floats may be of stainless steel or any material suitable for a particular application, with the shape designed to match requirements.

Piston Area Meters. These comprise a sleeve or cylinder held rigidly in a cast iron body, the cylinder having a closely fitting, honed, metering plug sliding in its bore. Rectangular metering slots or orifices are cut into the walls of the cylinder. Metering is achieved by the bottom edge of the plug lip and the slots in the cyinder wall, the plug rising and exposing a greater port area to the fluid as the flow increases. Plugs may be of stainless steel with hardened edges. Adjustment of capacity range is by means of a balancing spring, and indication is by an extension rod and indicator or transducer. (Fig. 45b)

POSITIVE DISPLACEMENT METERS

Fig. 46 shows a positive displacement type meter. These take many forms, including gear types, lobe types and the vane type. The Avery-Hardoll vane type is shown in the figure, which indicates the liquid flow which, by impingement on the blades, causes the rotor to move in a clockwise direction. The rotor provides a seal against the wall of the working chamber at the inlet, whilst the blades are kept in contact with the working chamber surface by the fluid pressure, trifugal force and gravity. The blades are free to slide on the rods. Accuracies in the region of $0 \cdot 1\%$ from maximum down to $0 \cdot 1$ of maximum flow are claimed for p.d. meters. Pipe bores of 200 mm can be accommodated with flows of approximately 12 litres/sec. This particular type can handle oil of viscosity in the region of 2500 secs Redwood No. 1 at $37 \cdot 8°C$ ($100°F$) and the quantity of the fluid measured per revolution varies according to size, but 2 litres to over 8 litres ($\frac{1}{2}$ to over $1\frac{1}{2}$ gall) is an approximate value. Various forms of indicator may be fitted including remote reading applications and materials can be adjusted for particular applications.

Where corrosive or hazardous fluids are involved, an enclosed meter with a magnetic pick-up may be employed. In most cases good upstream filtration is required.

TURBINE OR PROPELLER TYPE FLOWMETERS

The quantity of liquid flowing in a pipeline can be determined by the rate at which a propeller or turbine is made to rotate by the liquid flowing through a pipe. The assumptions are made that firstly so little force is required to operate the turbine that there is no slippage and secondly that the liquid will not change the flow and torque characteristics of the propeller. Two versions exist; one has a helical gear on the spindle which drives a pointer through a stuffing box and associated gearing. Vertical or horizontal forms are available. The rotor is often hollow and may be of plastic or a suitable material to match liquid requirements. The second version (Fig. 47) incorporates an electro-magnetic pick-up using a high speed rotor incorporating a magnet. The magnet is polarized at right-angles to the axis of rotation.

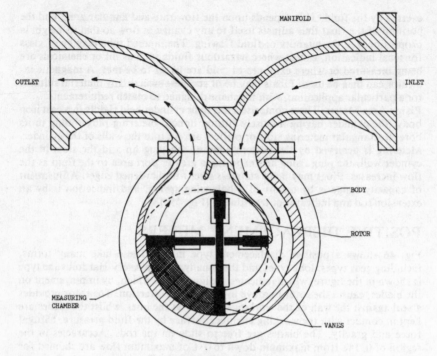

Fig. 46 Positive Displacement Meter

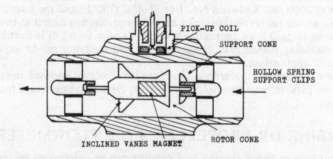

Fig. 47 Turbine Flowmeter

The rotor is shaped in the form of a cone, with the base upstream, and a cone is placed on the upstream bearing support so that the incoming fluid is initially subject to a velocity increase and pressure decrease. As the fluid passes along the tapering rotor there is a conversion of energy with a drop in velocity and increase in pressure, the latter, acting on the cone, tending to force the rotor upstream. The difference in rotor cone and support cone diameters has the effect of restricting this upstream movement. Friction between the liquid and rotor also produces a downstream force so that the rotor floats with minimum friction and no thrust bearings are required.

Upstream filtration should be provided, although flow will continue if the meter jams. Sizes range up to and over 400 mm pipe diameter with throughputs of about 160 litres/second. This second type is usually installed horizontally and on the pump outlet. The rate of rotation is proportional to flow rate and the electrical output signal can be used for control and indication purposes. The a.c. output lends itself to a digital counting system by measuring the pulses or, through a frequency converter, to a d.c. monitoring system.

ELECTROMAGNETIC FLOWMETERS (Fig. 48)

These may be used for measuring hazardous fluids, corrosive fluids or fluids with a high solids content, as on dredgers. Operation follows the basic electrical law in that when an electric conductor moves through a magnetic field in a direction perpendicular to its length, and also perpendicular to the lines of force, an electro-motive force is set up in the conductor which is proporitonal to the number of lines of force cut by the conductor in unit time. The relationship is:

$E = Bvd$

Where E is the e.m.f. in volts, d is the flux density of the magnetic field, v is the velocity of the conductor through the field, i.e., the fluid velocity, and d the length of the conductor, i.e., the pipe diameter or the diameter of a disc of fluid flowing through the pipe at any instant.

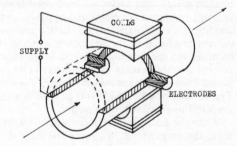

Fig. 48 Electro-magnetic Flowmeter

With a constant field strength, B, the fluid velocity is the only variable on the right hand side of the equation and thus the voltage generated is directly proportional to flow. Low flow velocities of approximately 0·75 m/sec can be measured, the signal output is linear and flow in either direction can be measured. The instrument tube is made of non-conducting, non-magnetic austenitic stainless steel, high electric resistivity being required so that the magnetic flux does not by-pass the fluid and to reduce eddy currents. The tube interior is lined with Neoprene to protect it and to prevent short circuiting of the generated voltage. The electrical potential is detected by two stainless steel or platinum electrodes, placed diametrically opposite each other, and alternating current is supplied to the magnets to prevent polarization of the electrodes.

CHAPTER 5

Miscellaneous Instruments

Shaft Power Meters. These meters are used to measure the power being transmitted by the propeller shaft from engine to propeller. The shaft being of an elastic material, twists under the influence of a torsional load such as that produced by propeller, the angular deflection produced being directly proportional to the torque transmitted. A constant for the shaft torque/twist relationship is a function of the shaft diameters (if hollow) and the modulus of rigidity of the shaft material;

$$T = \frac{JC}{L} \text{ where } T = \text{torque}$$

J = 2nd movement of Area of shaft section
L = Distance between reference points
C = Shaft material modulus of rigidity

Various types are in use; a very common one produced by AEI is shown in Fig. 49.

This particular instrument uses two identical transformers, one in the instrument casing the other with the cores on one shaft sleeve and the 'H' piece on the second shaft sleeve. The secondary windings of each transformer are wound in such a way that under no load conditions, with all the air gaps equal, the currents produced are equal and opposite. As the shaft twists under the loaded condition, the air gaps on the shaft transformer alter due to the twist and the current produced in the secondary winding of the transformer now no longer balances out the secondary current in the instrument transformer. The resultant current gives a reading on the meter. The instrument transformer is now adjusted until its air gaps match those of the shaft unit, and the meter reads zero. The amount of adjustment is then read in a formula with the shaft constant and the RPM to give shaft horse power.

When the device is used in conjunction with a data logger only the shaft unit is used, the output from this being fed directly to the logger. Another design uses the natural frequency of vibration of a stretched wire, which is proportional to the square of the stress applied. Fig. 50(a) shows the basic arrangement which involves two sensing wires being stretched between lugs fixed to two collars clamped on the shaft a given distance apart. When the shaft comes under load and twists, the angular deflection stretches one wire whilst the stress in the other is reduced. The wires are excited to vibrate at their natural frequency by an electronic control unit with a power frequency system in which the shaft itself forms part of the core of a transformer. The primary is stationary and the secondary wound round the shaft. Rectifiers mounted on the shaft provide a steady supply to the amplifiers etc. The effect of centrifugal force on the wires is self-cancelling, as are the effects of temperature, shaft bending and torsional vibration.

An *electro-magnet system* is used to transmit the mechanical vibration of the wires by transducing it to an electrical signal of the same frequency. These

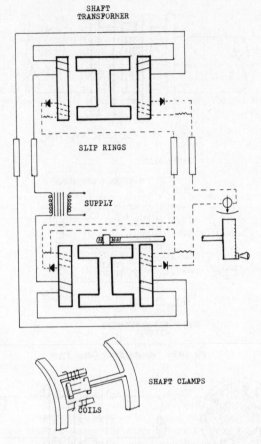

SHAFT
TRANSFORMER

SLIP RINGS

SUPPLY

SHAFT CLAMPS

COILS

Fig. 49 Variable Air Gap Transformer Meter

signals are then transmitted by radio frequency transmitters via circular aerials mounted on the shaft, with a receiver aerial mounted at the side of the shaft picking up the signal and transmitting it to a data-logger etc. This is an application of *unbonded strain gauges*.

Bonded strain gauges are used in the device in Fig. 50(b). Here the angular deformation of the propeller shaft caused by the torque is converted into a change in resistance of four strain gauges glued on the shaft. The strain gauges are fixed at an angle of 45° to the shaft centre line, along the lines of principal stress, and connected into a Wheatstone bridge circuit, with an e.m.f. applied across one diagonal and a measuring instrument connected across the other. In earlier systems the e.m.f. and the measurement signal were transmitted through brush gear on to slip rings, but in more modern systems the change in resistance is converted into a frequency change by means of a frequency converter fitted to the shaft with a contactless power supply. This is shown on the lower side of the diagram.

37

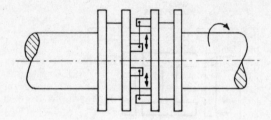

Fig. 50(a)   Unbonded Strain Gauge Type

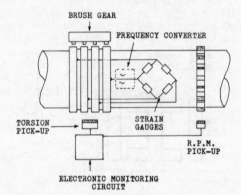

Fig. 50(b)   Bonded Strain Gauge Type

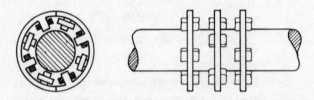

Fig. 50(c)   Magnetic Stress Sensitivity Type

The output of the converter is transmitted by an inductive antenna on the shaft, contactless to the digital frequency receiver. Speed sensing is by means of a toothed ring of ferromagnetic material which rotates within the field of an electro-magnetic pick up, varying its reluctance (magnetic resistance) and producing a series of impulses which are counted and produce a signal which is a function of the shaft speed.

Phase Lag Type. Two rings carrying a number of poles are mounted a given distance (about 1 metre) apart on the shaft. As the poles on the two rings pass stationary pick-ups, pulses are generated in the pick-up coils. As the shaft produces a greater angular deflection with increasing torque, so the pulses in the two pick-ups become more and more out of phase. To enable a measurement to be made of the torque, the pulses from the leading armature ring are used to open the electronic gate of a counting circuit, whilst the pulse from the lagging ring closes the gate. This counting circuit is thus open for a period determined by the shaft torque. The shaft speed measurement is carried out in a similar manner to that for the previous instrument and the output from this fed to the counting circuit. By feeding in the speed signal, the shaft power can be measured. Accuracy within 1 per cent is claimed.

Magnetic Stress Sensitivity Type or Torductor. (Fig. 50(c)). The operation of this type of device produced by ASEA, depends upon a physical effect that stress has upon the magnetization of some ferromagnetic materials. This effect depends on the material but for some, if a rod is put in tension, then magnetization in the direction of the stress is made easier, whilst magnetization across the stress lines is harder. Other materials are the reverse of this. In the Torductor, three rings are fitted around the shaft, each ring carrying the same number of electromagnetic poles with an air gap of approximately 3 mm between the shaft and the poles. The poles on the two outer rings are in line with each other and the centre ring has its poles mid-way between the others. Alternating current at 50 H$_z$ is supplied to the centre ring and a magnetic flux is set up which passes through the shaft between the two outer poles at 45° to the shaft axis. The coils on each of the outer rings are connected in series, but with the two complete windings in opposition. The arrangement now acts as a transformer with the centre ring as the primary and the outer rings as the secondary windings, whilst the shaft material completes the magnetic circuit. The reluctance or magnetic resistance of the shaft material under the no torque condition allows a symmetrical magnetic field around the rings and the net output is zero. As the torque is applied and the shaft comes under torsional stress, the reluctance changes as stresses are set up at 45° to the shaft axis (principal stress lines), reducing in one direction and increasing in the other so that the magnetic field is distorted. This distortion produces an e.m.f. in the outer coils which is a function of the torque in the shaft. By taking off this reading from the outer rings and combining it with a shaft speed reading, the shaft horse power can be found. This device does not depend upon shaft twist over a given length for operation.

Tachometers. Fig. 51(a) shows a *simple mechanical tachometer* employing a weighted arm or ball which moves out of position due to centrifugal force. This

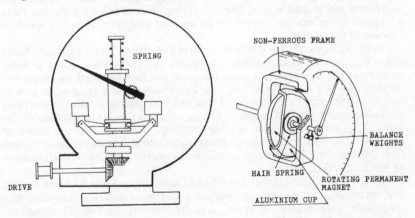

Fig. 51(a)   Tachometer (mechanical)   Fig. 51(b)   Tachometer (magnetic drag)

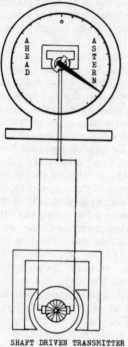

SHAFT DRIVEN TRANSMITTER

Fig. 51(c)   Tachometer (electric d.c.)

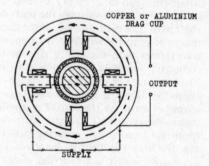

COPPER or ALUMINIUM DRAG CUP

OUTPUT

SUPPLY

Fig. 52 Tachometer (a.c.)

movement of the arms operates the pointer over the rpm scale. It operates in the same direction for ahead and astern running. Fig. 51(b) shows a magnetic drag tachometer in which the effect of the rotating magnetic field is to drag the aluminium cup around with it. The hair spring opposes this but sufficient force is applied to deflect the pointer by an amount proportional to the speed of rotation of the magnet.

Electric tachometers are used with control and distant reading circuitry being either d.c. or a.c. tachogenerators driven by the shaft whose speed is being measured. The d.c. type is a generator with the flux provided by permanent magnets, using a wound armature with a commutator and designed to give an output voltage directly proportional to speed. The output is taken to a moving coil instrument calibrated in rpm. When no current is flowing, the pointer of this meter is positioned by two opposing springs, with zero at the centre of the scale. The direction of the shaft rotation controls the direction of current flow through the coil and hence the pointer shows the direction of shaft rotation as well as rpm (Fig. 51c))

The a.c. type dispenses with brushes and commutators and by using a 'drag cup' technique, can be made to produce a voltage at constant frequency with magnitude proportional to speed, angular velocity or rate of change of displacement (Fig. 52). The stator carries two windings with their axes at 90° to one another, one being the supply coil, the other the pick-up or output coil. The rotor consists of a thin aluminium or copper cup rotating about a soft iron core. When the cup is stationary, there is no output as the coils are at 90°. If, when the cup is being rotated at constant speed, a d.c. supply is provided to the input coil, e.m.f's will be induced by the generator action, but the effect is to produce an interacting flux behaviour so that there is no output. Acceleration of shaft rpm and thus cup rotational speed however produces an output voltage in the coils.

If a.c. is supplied to the input coil, the main flux alternates at the supply frequency. Induced e.m.f.'s in the cup due to its rotation, cutting the supply coil flux, link with the output coil producing a signal proportional to the speed of rotation in this coil, with the frequency and phase that of the supply.

The magnetic pulse generator is frequently used with load sensing governors and power meters. It has been described in the section on torque meters.

WATER PURITY METERS

Salinity Indicator (Crockett) (Fig. 53(a)). The basic principle behind the operation of this very commonly used instrument is the fact that pure water has a very high electrical resistance and therefore a very low conductivity, to the extent that absolutely pure water can be considered as non-conductive. If sea-water is

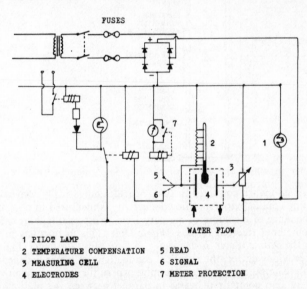

1 PILOT LAMP
2 TEMPERATURE COMPENSATION   5 READ
3 MEASURING CELL   6 SIGNAL
4 ELECTRODES   7 METER PROTECTION

Fig. 53(a) and (b) overleaf   Salinity Indicators

added to pure water, the resistance to the passage of an electric current fails, i.e. the conductivity increases. This instrument measures the conductivity of water such as in boiler feed systems by passing a sample through a small cell containing two platinum electrodes and measuring the current flow that occurs due to the conductance effect of any salts present. Readings are based on the assumption that the conductivity is due to sodium chloride (N_aCl) or Cl as the case may be, but other salts such as magnesium chloride and calcium chloride will almost certainly be present. It is assumed for convenience that all conductivity is due to sodium chloride, and although this is not strictly accurate, it is sufficiently so for practical purposes. Its conductivity has been investigated over a very wide range of concentration and temperature and is thus a convenient standard for comparison.

The electrical conductivity of water rises with temperature, about $2 \cdot 2$ per cent per °C, and therefore a mercury in glass thermometer is used to adjust the current flow for this. As the mercury rises under an increase in temperature, it shorts out the resistances and leaks off an appropriate value of current commensurate with the temperature variation from the indicator and alarm circuit. Readings are in grains of salt per gallon, conductivity units or reciprocal megohms/cm^3, microhms/cm^3.

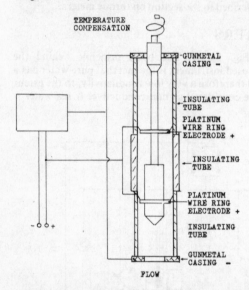

Fig. 53(b)

This last unit when corrected to 20°C provides numerically convenient values representing conductivity (specific conductivity is measured in ohm/cm^3 and is the conductance of a column of mercury 1 cm^3 cross sectional area, 1 cm long) and is sometimes referred to as a *Dionic* Unit. This in turn has provided the name for the *Dionic Water Purity Meter*, or flow tube type meter (Fig. 53(b)). As with the previous device, the electrical conductivity of water is dependent upon the dissolved impurities and to determine where the meter measures the conductivity of two columns of water in parallel between the platinum and gun metal collars. The insulating plunger operated by the bi-metal strip temperature compensator automatically varies the water flow to give compensation to 20°C. Dissolved Co_2 can produce errors and should be removed by de-gasifiers.

Other designs utilize two electrodes in a suitably perforated probe which screws into a pipe line, the operating principal being similar to the previous instruments, with leads taken from the electrodes to measuring and alarm circuits. It is important that the measuring electrodes are kept very clean and electrical connections sound.

pH Meter. The reason for measuring the pH value of a solution such as water in a boiler or boiler feed system, is to ascertain whether it is likely to cause corrosion either by being acid or strongly alkaline. This is done by measuring the concentration of hydrogen ions actually dissociated in the water and comparing the value obtained with a scale indicating degrees of acidity and alkalinity (0–14, strong acid to strong alkaline respectively, 7 being neutral). A continuous reading meter for this purpose depends for its operation upon the development of an e.m.f. across a thin membrane of special types of glass, this e.m.f. being directly related to the difference in hydrogen concentration between the solutions separated by the membrane. In this instrument the membrane is in the form of a glass bulb (Fig. 54) containing a solution which has a constant pH value (known as a buffer solution—could be Potassium Chloride). Connection with this liquid is through a silver electrode coated with silver chloride forming an electrical junction with a stable potential. Such an electrode in a solution of a given hydrogen ion concentration on one side of such a membrane is sensitive to changes in the hydrogen ion concentration on the other side. A connection from this electrode or half cell to the meter forms one pole of the measuring unit.

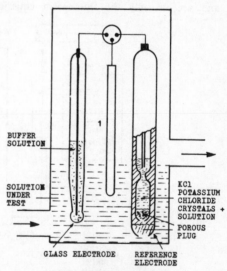

Fig. 54 pH Meter

BUFFER SOLUTION

SOLUTION UNDER TEST

1

KCl POTASSIUM CHLORIDE CRYSTALS + SOLUTION

POROUS PLUG

GLASS ELECTRODE   REFERENCE ELECTRODE

1 TEMPERATURE COMPENSATION

In order to measure the voltage developed in the glass membrane or bulb, a reference cell is used and connection with the outer surface of the glass bulb is made through the solution under test and a liquid junction. This is a solution of potassium chloride in a glass tube with a porous plug in the bottom, and develops a very low and stable liquid junction potential with the sample solution, as long as a very slight flow of potassium chloride solution with the sample is maintained. The reference cell is in contact with the potassium chloride through another porous plug and forms a stable e.m.f. here. The reference cell and the potassium chloride are together known as the reference electrode, and this has a constant e.m.f. regardless of the hydrogen ion concentration around it. The glass or measuring electrode produces an e.m.f. proportional to the difference in the hydrogen ion concentration between the solution in the tube (constant pH) and that of the liquid being checked, and thus the difference in the electrical potential between the glass measuring electrode and the reference electrode measures the pH of the solution.

As temperature affects the disassociation of hydrogen, temperature compensation has to be provided by a thermometer immersed in the solution.

Accuracy can be affected by dampness, strong electric fields, dirty electrodes, distorted electrodes, poor electrical connections, incorrect installation (holes in the glass cover should face flow). If glass electrodes dry out they may not give correct reading unless soaked in buffer solution for 24 hours).

Oil in Water Monitor. This is used to check for oil contamination of bilges or ballast water after the separator; also boiler feed water. The device shown in Fig. 55 produced by Bailey Meters and Controls Ltd, operates on the principle of ultra violet fluorescence. This is the phenomenon of the emission of light from a molecule or atom which has absorbed light of one particular wave length and re-emits some of this energy at a longer wavelength. A primary light filter allows only the required ultra-violet wavelength on to the sample and excludes all others, whilst a secondary or emission filter cuts back this excitation wavelength and accepts only the fluorescent emission wavelength. These wavelengths

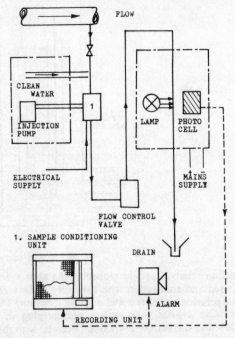

Fig. 55 Oil in Water Monitor

passing the latter filter are detected by a photo-electric cell. The output of this is a measure of the fluorescence and hence the oil contamination.

A sample is taken from the main flow line and passed through a conditioning unit to reduce the dispersed particles to a constant size (5 microns or less) and this ensures the highest efficiency. Flow then continues through a flow control valve to the sensor unit where, if there are any oil particles present, the ultra violet light causes fluorescence in these. A photo electric cell then picks up any light present due to the fluorescence of the oil and produces an electrical signal which is thus a function of the oil contamination of the water.

In order to prevent dust and condensation fouling the glass, an air purge is provided, and the mixture passes through the sensor in the form of a falling jet. The instrument has to be calibrated for a particular oil or against a sample of given oil-water mixture. The monitor is suitable for a wide range of oils and can monitor concentration 0–30 up to 0–6000 ppm depending upon oil type.

Photo Electric Cells. The energy radiated by a beam of light is used in these cells to provide a means of control and alarm in a very wide variety of applications such as oil mist detectors, flame failure devices and oil in water detectors. The effect of the light energy on the cell depends upon the materials used in the construction. In *photo-emissive* cells as shown in Fig. 56(a), visible light rays are caused by positioning the cell or light appropriately, to fall on a film of metal such as Caesium and the light energy this absorbs allows electrons to escape from the surface and accelerates them towards an anode forming part of an electrical circuit. The cell consists of a glass envelope, under vacuum conditions inside (evacuated), enclosing a large photo-sensitive surface area acting as a cathode, and a small rod of wire acting as the anode and shielding the cathode as little as possible from the light source. If the anode and cathode are connected into an electrical circuit producing a sufficiently intense electric field between them, the photo-electrons emitted from the cathode will accelerate towards the anode and a photo-current will flow in the external anode circuit. This circuit receives electrons from the anode and delivers them to the cathode to replace those lost by photo-emission.

An inert gas filled type is also available in which the gas is ionized by the emitted electrons, producing more electrons and the photo-currents can be amplified by 3 to 10 times. This design is, however, subject to temperature change effects.

Photo Conductive Cells employ semi-conductor materials such as selenium, germanium and silicon, as the light sensing medium. These materials have the property of varying their electrical resistance when light falls on them. The cells have a very thin layer of the semi-conductor exposed to the light, the layer acting as a variable resistor with its resistance altering as the amount of light reaching it varies. These are suitable for infra-red light sensing.

Photo-voltaic cells are constructed as shown in Fig. 56(b). Photo-currents are generated near the cadmium/selenium interface, as the former material has a strong attraction for electrons and collects those released by the impact of light on the selenium. No power supply is required by this type but age fatigue is a problem and they are temperature sensitive. With some flame failure applications, discrimination between the flames of a number of adjacent burners has created problems when one flame has extinguished. Fig. 56(c) shows an attempt to overcome this problem.

Viscosity Sensor (Viscometer). To obtain a continuous reading of viscosity of a fluid such as oil fuel for an IC engine, an application of the theory covering isothermal laminar flow in circular tubes has to be considered and this involves a constant quantity of oil supplied under isothermal conditions and laminar flow to a capillary tube of constant cross section area and given length. Under these conditions the viscosity becomes a linear function of the pressure drop across the capillary tube. This theory is the basis of the design of the VAF Viscotherm

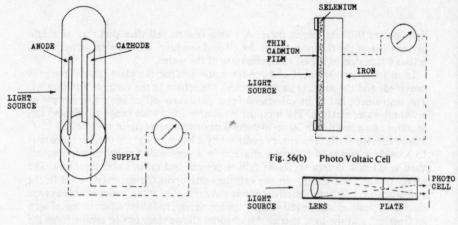

Fig. 56(a)　　Photo Emissive Cell

Fig. 56(b)　　Photo Voltaic Cell

Fig. 56(c)　　Discrimination Tube

shown in Fig. 57. Here a constant quantity of oil is taken from the flow into the meter and supplied by a precision gear pump, driven at 40 rpm by an electric motor via reduction gears, to a capillary tube through which it flows under laminar (streamline) conditions. (Laminar flow indicates that there are no cross currents or eddies). The pressure drop across the tube is measured by a d.p. cell and the signal obtained is directly proportional to the viscosity of the oil. This signal may then be used to operate a control system adjusting the steam valve to an oil fuel heater. The unit should be placed as near as possible to the heater discharge. All parts are of stainless steel.

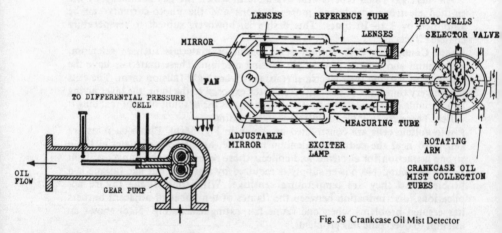

Fig. 58 Crankcase Oil Mist Detector

Fig. 57 VAF Viscometer

Oil Mist Detector (Graviner). This instrument, shown in Fig. 58, is used to sample the air/oil mixture in a diesel engine crankcase and detect any concentrations due to a hot bearing etc., well below the level at which an explosion may occur. Oil mist is drawn into the instrument by a fan, driven by an electric motor, through sampling tubes connected to the top of the respective crank chambers of the crankcase. A rotating sampling valve, driven off the fan motor, connects each tube in turn for four seconds to the measuring tube, whilst a reference tube has a sample from the remaining crank chambers passing through it so that it can evaluate the difference in oil mist level. The overall mist density of all the crank chambers is also taken once every revolution of the sampling valve and compared with fresh air. A beam of light from a common lamp is reflected by mirrors along the axis of the parallel measuring and reference tubes, energizing silicon photo electric cells connected electrically back to back, so that the output from the circuit is the difference between their individual currents.

Under normal conditions the oil mist level is the same in both tubes and the output is zero. An increase in oil mist density in any one crank chamber will unbalance the photo-cell output and at a predetermined level an alarm is energized. A rotating indicator stops at the crank chamber with the abnormal oil mist condition. The lenses and cells should be cleared periodically and the circuits tested daily. The connecting tubes should slope and have no loops to prevent oil blockage. Another version is available in which each crank chamber is compared with a fresh air sample.

Vibration Monitors. Vibration monitoring is being used quite extensively as a means of detecting malfunctioning of rotating machinery at an early stage—long before failure occurs.

Two types of measurement are made, the amplitude (i.e. displacement velocity or acceleration of the component being monitored) and the frequency at which it occurs. The former gives an indication of condition and the latter identifies the probable source. Two instruments are used for these purposes. One, as shown in Fig. 59(a), is a velocity transducer. It consists basically of a coil surrounding a permanent magnet with the vibration of the machine causing the coil to oscillate relative to the magnet, thus converting the vibration of the machine into an electrical signal. This is proportional to the velocity and can be used to indicate displacement by an integrating amplifier.

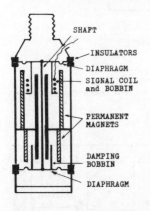

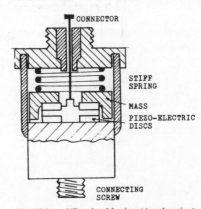

Fig. 59(a)   Vibration Monitor (Velocity)   Fig. 59(b)   Vibration Monitor (Acceleration)

Fig. 59(b) shows an accelerometer based on the piezo-electric cell. The instrument comprises a number of discs of piezo-electric crystals beneath a heavy mass. This assembly is then mounted on a heavily sprung loaded base and sealed in a metal case. When vibrated the mass exerts a force on the piezo-electric discs and these generate an electrical signal directly proportional to the force applied and therefore to the acceleration of the mass. By the use of integrating circuits, velocity or displacement interpretations can be displayed.

Piezo-electric cells consist of discs of certain types of crystals such as tourmaline or quartz, which when electrically deformed along certain stress planes, produce an electrical potential between opposite faces. Electrodes attached to these faces measure these charges. The crystals give a very rapid response to changes in pressure.

GAS ANALYSIS

Oxygen. Reduction of uptake corrosion and monitoring combustion efficiency are two important reasons for checking the oxygen content of boiler uptakes, while gas used for inerting cargo tanks in oil tankers has to be kept to about 3–5 per cent (alarm at 8 per cent) to ensure the tank atmosphere is inert.

A number of methods can be used. Fig. 60(a) shows an *electro-chemical type* analyser whilst Fig. 60(b) shows a magnetic wind (thermo-magnetic type). In the former a high temperature galvanic cell is used consisting of a calcium stabilized zirconium oxide electrolyte with platinum electrodes. These cells require to be heated to about 800°C, when the oxygen molecules on the anode (the side of the cell exposed to a high oxygen partial pressure) gain electrons. At the same time oxygen molecules are formed by reverse action on the cathode.

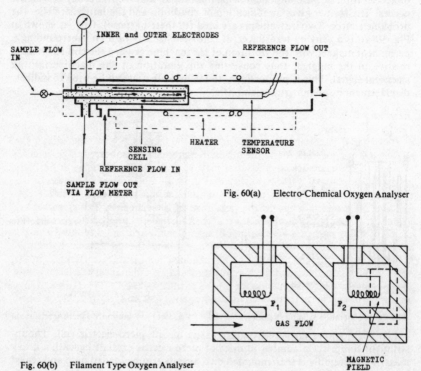

INNER and OUTER ELECTRODES

SAMPLE FLOW IN

REFERENCE FLOW OUT

SENSING CELL

HEATER

TEMPERATURE SENSOR

REFERENCE FLOW IN

SAMPLE FLOW OUT VIA FLOW METER

Fig. 60(a)   Electro-Chemical Oxygen Analyser

F_1 F_2

GAS FLOW

MAGNETIC FIELD

Fig. 60(b)   Filament Type Oxygen Analyser

Output is unaffected by CO_2 or water and the response is very fast. The e.m.f. generated can be used to operate a meter, and a supply of clean dry air is used as a reference.

The *magnetic wind type* depends for its operation upon the fact that oxygen is rare among gasses in that it is paramagnetic, i.e. it is attracted by a magnetic field, but the effect is inversely proportional as the square of the oxygen temperature, decreasing rapidly as the temperature increases.

In the *filament type* shown, two platinum filaments F_1 and F_2 are mounted in cavities in a metal block, each open to the gas stream being analysed. An electric current heats the filaments which form two arms of a Wheatstone Bridge. Filament F_2 has a magnetic field passed across it, the field only crossing part of the filament and its associated heated zone. Thus the oxygen in the gas sample is attracted into the cooler zone of the field, but as it passes across the heater it loses its attraction into the field rapidly and the pressure difference induces a gas flow. This flow of gas cools filament F_2, altering the relationship to F_1, and unbalancing the Wheatstone Bridge. In turn a recorder is operated. It is important to maintain constant temperatures and pressures; $1\,^{\circ}C$ temperature change can give a $1\frac{1}{2}$ per cent change in reading.

A third type of instrument, the *magneto dynamic*, is based on two spheres filled with nitrogen which is diamagnetic (repelled by a magnetic field). The spheres are fixed at the ends of a box forming a dumb-bell supported on a torsion bar suspension. The whole cell operates inside a strong non-uniform magnetic field, the spheres being repelled from the strongest part, rotating the suspension until this force is balanced by the torsion of the suspension. When the oxygen content changes, the force on the dumb-bell alters and it takes up a new position. In a practical application a variable electro-magnetic field is used to balance the force on the dumb-bell, holding it in zero position and the current to produce this field measures the oxygen content of the gas. A portable version has Lloyds approval.

Various types of meter may be used for measuring the CO_2 content of flue gases and thus ensure that good combustion of the oil in a boiler furnace is taking place. Fig. 61(a) shows a continuous reading type in which platinum wire elements are mounted in two chambers, one the measuring chamber with a gas sample passing through it and the other, the reference chamber, with air passing through it. (In some designs the latter may be sealed.) The elements are usually contained in a heavy block to ensure that the wall temperatures of the cells are the same. Operation depends upon the relative thermal conductivity of CO_2 and air, and the effect this has on the resistance of the elements. The elements are heated to a high temperature relative to the cell walls by an electric current, the circuit forming part of a Wheatstone Bridge. The filtered and dried uniform gas and air flows are drawn across the elements and the difference in thermal conductivity of the CO_2 relative to air causes a temperature difference in the wires and hence a change in the wire resistance. This unbalances the Wheatstone Bridge and the degree of unbalance is used to indicate the CO_2 present. CO_2 has an approximate thermal conductivity of 1 against CO of 4, O_2 of 2, N_2 of 2 and H_2O of 1 (hence the need for drying). Any CO or H_2 present is recorded as CO_2 unless previously removed.

In the *absorption type*, when the gas containing CO_2 is brought into contact with a KOH (Potassium Hydroxide) solution, the following reaction takes place:
$$CO_2 + 2KOH \qquad K_2CO_3 + H_2O$$

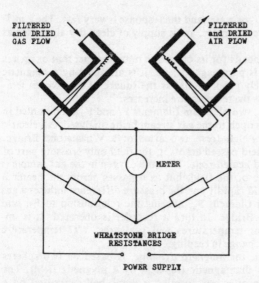

FILTERED and DRIED GAS FLOW

FILTERED and DRIED AIR FLOW

METER

WHEATSTONE BRIDGE RESISTANCES

POWER SUPPLY

Fig. 61(a) CO_2 Meter

The volume of gas remaining will be reduced by a percentage equal to the equal volume percentage of CO_2. This type usually involves a filter in the line to a tube containing the liquid. A given volume of gas is pumped into the tube, displacing the air, and then the gas and liquid mixed. The change in level of the liquid is an indication of the volume of CO_2 absorbed.

Carbon Dioxide recorders also form an essential part of the equipment necessary for the successful carriage of fruit cargoes and other perishable foodstuffs.

DETECTION OF EXPLOSIVE GASES

Catalytic combustion devices are probably the most commonly used monitors for checking flammable compounds in the atmosphere. They incorporate a thermopile, thermistor or a self-heated hot-wire detector, with platinum being one of the metals used in the last device, and possibly being heated to maintain a temperature of about $65°C$. Two such detectors are incorporated into a Wheatstone Bridge circuit, the hot catalytic detector causing the combustibles to burn in the presence of oxygen. Should there not be an excess of oxygen present, oxygen or air has to be added in controlled amounts to provide an excess to the extent that the reaction is limited by the amount of combustibles present. When the mixture burns heat is released which is detected as a temperature rise in the catalytic detector filament, and as the resistance of this is a function of its temperature, any fluctuation in the latter causes a variation in the former. This unbalances the bridge, the variation being proportional to the concentration of the combustibles. The device does not differentiate between various gases but gives a combined output for the mixture in question. The reference detector can be exposed either to a suitable reference gas such as air or to the sample, the catalytic characteristic being destroyed by poisoning or coating. The latter compensates for thermal conductivity change in the sample caused by changing sample conditions. The complete unit is usually built into a small box with the sensing element in a gas chamber. An aspirator bulb is used to draw in an air/gas sample and if gas is present the heat of combustion unbalances the Wheatstone Bridge circuit which in turn operates a meter scaled to read in percentage lower explosive limit. Both portable and permanent continuous or intermittent readout, multi-point, devices are available.

The non-dispersive infra-red gas analyser consists of two filaments of nickel-chrome alloy which provide a source of infra-red energy. They are heated to about $800°C$ and the energy stream emanating from them is then blocked by an opaque disc or chopper, a disc pierced by equally spaced holes and rotated in the energy stream by an electric motor. Pulses of energy are thus produced with equal on-off periods down to frequencies of about 2Hz. The energy streams then pass through filters into two cells, one a sample cell comprising a highly polished tube conducting the energy stream continuously along its length by multiple reflection. The other is the reference cell or tube and is used to transmit the energy through an inert gas. The energy streams then pass into a sealed chamber incorporating a very thin highly flexible diaphragm which separates the two sections exposed to the energy beam. This chamber contains the same gas as the component to be measured in the sample stream together with an inert gas for improved sensitivity. This gas sensitizes the analyser to the desired component of the gas stream to be detected and absorbs radiation at wavelengths limited to those that the sample absorbs. If the sample cell or tube pulse is attenuated (reduced) by absorption of the infra-red energy of the gas in the sample tube, the relative pressure between the two chambers is altered and the diaphragm deflects. The diaphragm forms a capacitance plate in an electric capacitance bridge network and thus any variation in capacitance can be amplified to give a continuous output signal proportional to the gas concentration (Fig. 61(b)).

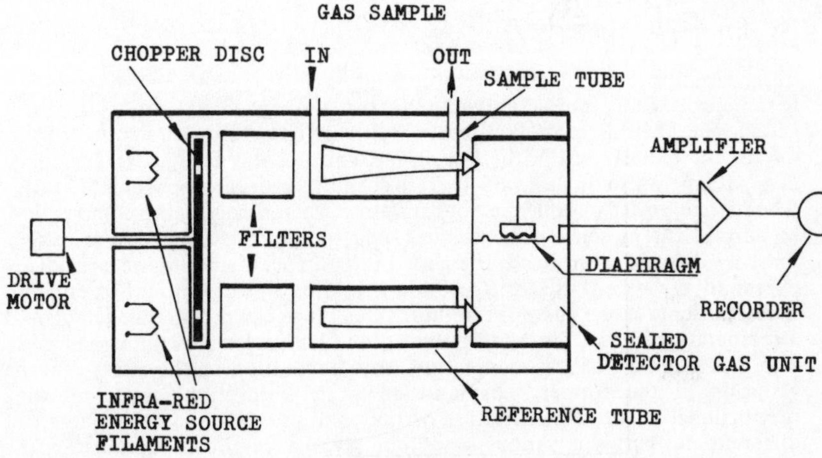

Fig. 61(b)

CHAPTER 6

Signal Transmitting Devices

In the previous chapters the various means for detecting and measuring changes in pressures, temperatures, levels and flows were examined. Many of these devices, such as bourdon tubes, bellows, filled system thermometers etc., are only suitable for local or comparatively short distance remote visual monitoring and in their basic form cannot be used for automatic control, alarm or data logging or for acquisition purposes.

This chapter explains some of the devices used to produce signals suited to long distance signal transmission for control, alarm and recording purposes. The process may generally be named *telemetering* and the devices are often called *transducers*. The definition of a transducer is generally considered to cover a device which produces an electrical output signal proportional to an applied physical stimulus, for example a force or displacement. This definition has been stretched somewhat to cover such devices as the pneumatic signal transmitters shown in Fig. 62(a).

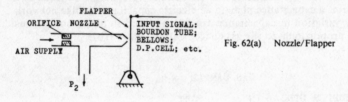

Fig. 62(a)   Nozzle/Flapper

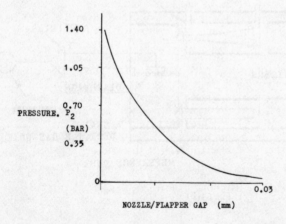

Fig. 62(b)   Air Gap/Pressure Relationship

Flapper Nozzle. Air is fed to the nozzle at a constant pressure via a restrictor (to limit air flow so that P_2 is approximately atmospheric pressure when the nozzle/flapper gap is maximum). The air leaks to atmosphere at a rate depending upon the clearance beween the flapper and the nozzle tip and follows the curve shown in Fig. 62(b). With the flapper hard on the nozzle P_2 (the back pressure) would be $1 \cdot 4$ bar (20 psi) whilst if it is moved away approximately $0 \cdot 03$ mm, P_2 is then only slightly above atmospheric. As the curve shows, the back pressure P_2 flapper movement relationship is only approximately linear over the signal range, but if the curve is taken between the P_2 pressures of $0 \cdot 2$ bar and $0 \cdot 5$ bar, approximately $0 \cdot 015$ mm flapper travel, then the curve is much closer to the linear requirement. 'Linear' means that P_2 varies an equal amount each time the flapper moves an equal amount.

To achieve such sensitivity *Negative Feedback* has to be used as shown in the *Position Balance Transmitter* in Fig. 63. Feedback means, as the name implies, passing back the whole or part of the output signal into the device producing that signal. Here P_2 is fed back to the flapper through a bellows, with a spring to provide the requisite balancing force. Suppose the signal initially moving the

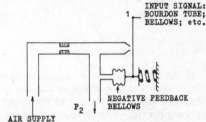

Fig. 63 Negative Feedback

flapper is provided by a bourdon tube at the end of a filled systems thermometer capillary tube. Assume the temperature at the bulb increases by 2°C and this causes the bourdon tube tip to move the flapper towards the nozzle by $0 \cdot 015$ mm. In Fig. 62, with no feedback, this movement would occupy the whole linear range so that P_2 changes from $0 \cdot 2$ bar to $0 \cdot 5$ bar and this would be the output signal, the instrument thus having a range of $0 \cdot 5$—$0 \cdot 2$ bar i.e. $0 \cdot 3$ bar for a 2°C temperature range. If the same temperature change is considered in Fig. 63 where negative feedback is applied, the flapper initially moves the same amount and the back pressure P_2 increases to $0 \cdot 5$ bar; but in doing so it causes the bellows to expand, pivoting the flapper about point 1. The nozzle/flapper gap then increases, moving it back towards, but not exactly to, its original position until a position of equilibrium is reached. The actual resultant movement of the flapper from its original position may then be only $0 \cdot 00025$ mm and the output (back pressure) will have increased by a very small amount, say $\cdot 05$ bar so that the output is now $0 \cdot 25$ bar. Thus with 2°C giving a pressure change of $\cdot 05$ bar, the temperature range that can be measured and transmitted has been increased to $0 \cdot 5 - \dfrac{0 \cdot 2}{0 \cdot 05} \times 2°C = 12°C$. The reason the feedback is given a negative notation is that it moves the flapper back towards its original position. If it moved the flapper even further away from its original position it would be called *positive feedback*. Any variable signal, level, pressure, flow etc., could be used to move the flapper, the position of point 1 being adjustable to suit the input movement available to give the flapper/nozzle the necessary gap variation for correct operation.

The nozzle/flapper described above may be considered as an amplifier, as a small input movement is converted in a measurable pneumatic signal, but the increments of pressure change are still too small to be transmitted over long distance or operate large equipment, and there is therefore a second stage amplifier (Fig. 64 (a and b). This may be called a booster or pilot valve relay. Here the nozzle back pressure acts on a diaphragm attached to a spindle with a valve on the opposite end. The leafspring can be adjusted to give the correct operating range and balance the load on the diaphragm. Air at input pressure, say 1·4 bar, is supplied to the underside of the ball valve.

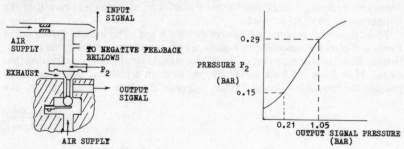

Fig. 64(a)   Pilot Valve Amplifier   Fig. 64(b)   Input/Output Pressure Relationship

If the back pressure P_2 increases as the flapper approaches the nozzle, the diaphragm pressure increases and the conical exhaust valve moves towards its seat, thus reducing the air bleeding off to atmosphere and at the same time opening the ball valve so that the output pressure increases. If the exhaust valve is shut in completely, the output pressure increases to 1·4 bar. If P_2 decreases, the spring moves the spindle to open the exhaust valve and shut in the ball valve reducing the output pressure to the extent that it drops to just above atmospheric if the ball valve shuts completely. Intermediate positions of the valves give output pressures from 0 to 1·4 bar.

The nozzle back pressure relationship with the pilot valve outlet is not linear over the full range and usually pilot valves are adjusted to accommodate a nozzle back pressure range of approximately 0·2 bar to 0·5 bar, a 0·3 bar range, which gives reasonable linearity for the nozzle/flapper behaviour. This gives an output range for the ball valve between 0·2 bar to 1·0 bar which is also approximately linear. Thus the diaphragm/ball valve amplifier increases the range of the output signal so that it can be used to operate other equipment over long distances and improves the linearity of the system.

The amplification gain or pressure range multiplcation factor is the diaphragm pressure range (P_2 range) divided into the ball valve output pressure range i.e.,

$(1·0-0·2)-(0·5-0·2) = \dfrac{0·8}{0·3}$ or approx. 2·6. These figures may vary according to manufacturer. This is said to be a direct acting device, i.e., as P_2 increases so the output increases pressure from the 2nd stage amplifier increases. If this latter pressure were to drop as P_2 increases it would be called a Reverse Acting device. Nozzles and flappers are kept small and light and orifices and nozzle diameters small, to keep air supply capacities down and reduce inertia and operating power requirements.

Fig. 63 is known as a *Position* or *Motion Balance Transmitter*. Fig. 65 shows a device operating on the *Force Balance* relationship. Here a bourdon tube, bellows, diaphragm etc., acts on the end of a beam as shown. The beam is pivoted, and at the opposite end to the applied force acts against a nozzle. Air is supplied through a restriction to a nozzle whence it bleeds to atmosphere. Any

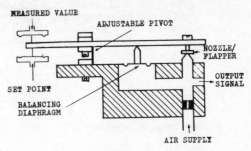

Fig. 65 Motion Balance Device

change in the measured condition of the system being monitored, alters the measured value signal and the difference between this and the set point signal pivots the right hand side altering the nozzle/flapper gap. Suppose the beam approaches the nozzle, then the air escape is restricted and the back pressure builds up, increasing the output pressure and also the force on the feedback diaphragm which in turn produces an opposing torque on the beam, tending to move it away from the flapper—having negative feed back effect.

A position of equilibrium is then set up so that the change in output pressure is proportional to the change in the signal representing the condition being monitored. On instruments of this type used in practice the position of the pivot is variable to alter the operating range and a zero adjusting spring is also fitted to create a force against the beam to pre-load it to give an output of 0·2 bar at the lowest value of the range over which the system is being monitored. The movement of the flapper is very small—about 0·025 mm. A diaphragm, ball valve type amplifier is usually fitted to improve the output signal as in the previous device. The device is less susceptible to vibration effect than the motion balance type.

An Electro-Pneumatic signal converter is shown in Fig. 66. The operation of this device is based on the force balance principle and consists of a permanent magnet situated between two pole pieces, with a pair of coils, connected to the input signal around an armature pivoted on a torsion bar held between fixed supports. Consider an increase in the d.c. milli-ampere input signal to the coils, which in turn increases the magnetic field, surrounding them, thus increasing the magnetic strength in the armature, and the magnetic attraction across the air gap between the armature and the pole pieces. These are already polarized by the permanent magnet. With the armature polarity as shown, the magnetic attraction forces the armature at the nozzle end up at the negative feed back bellows, like poles repelling, unlike poles attracting. The armature twists about the torsion rod supports, and moves closer to the nozzle, restricting the air flow and increasing the back pressure and output pressure. The increasing back pressure acts on the negative feedback bellows, which creates an equalizing force on the armature moving it back to an equilibrium position, with the output

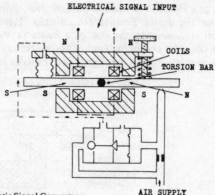

Fig. 66 Electro-pneumatic Signal Converter

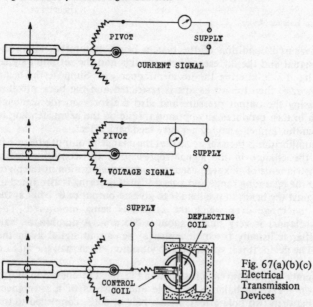

Fig. 67(a)(b)(c)
Electrical
Transmission
Devices

pressure acts on the negative feedback bellows, which creates an equalizing force on the armature moving it back to an equilibrium position, with the output pressure at a new value representing the electrical input signal. The reverse procedure occurs if the input signal falls. This is a direct acting device, reverse acting forms are available. Devices of this nature are used with electrical control systems to convert to a pneumatic signal for driving diaphragm operated valves or piston operated dampers. These can be cheaper and more easily positioned than electrically operated versions.

Electrical Signal Transmission. Two simple and cheap versions are shown in Figs. 67(a and b) the former giving mA signals and the latter mV signals. As the bourdon tube, bellows or float moves the arm it moves across a resistance, varying the amperes or volts in the circuit respectively. Problems can arise

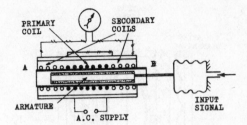

Fig. 68 Variable Inductance Transducer

through dirt, vibration and variation in voltage supply affecting indication, however the cross coil design in Fig. 67(c) eliminates this. The control coil is supply energized, its current thus being proportional to the supply voltage, whilst the current in the other coil depends upon the position of the sliding contact, and hence the condition of the system being monitored. The deflection depends entirely on voltage/current relationship.

Variable Inductance Type. A version of this is shown in Fig. 68. Here three coils are wound on a hollow former inside which a steel armature is moved by a bourdon tube, bellows, valve stem or similar device. The centre coil is the primary one and receives an a.c. supply, and the alternating current through this coil creates a fluctuating magnetic fied in the armature. The armature links this field to the outer coils, the amount of flux cutting these coils depending upon the position of the armature in the core. When it is in the centre both coils get equal flux distribution, when it is to the left coil A is predominant and when to the right coil B is predominant. The coils are wound in opposition so that the e.m.f. produced by the flux cutting coil A opposes that produced by coil B. Thus when the armature is in the centre e.m.f.'s induced in the coils balance out, while if the armature is to the left the e.m.f. in coil A is greater, and when to the right the e.m.f. in coil B is greater. The resultant output is a function of the condition being monitored. Such devices may also be known as *mutual inductance elements, differential transformers* or *inductance ratio devices.*

This device places no friction load on the measuring device. It has a linear response to a linear input, does not require special power supplies and is small and rugged needing no critical mounting adjustment or tolerances. With a bourdon tube or bellows imput it can be used for measuring pressures and with a filled system thermometer for measuring temperatures in a wide range of systems.

Variable Capacitance Transducer. Fig. 69 shows a variable capacity transducer application for measuring flow. The differential pressure across the orifice is fed to the isolating diaphragm on each side of the unit, which in turn transmits the pressure to a silicone oil filling inside the sensing unit. The oil exerts a high and low pressure on opposite sides of a sensing diaphragm in the centre of the unit, displacement of this diaphragm being proportional to the pressure difference across it. The position of this diaphragm is detected by capacitor plates on both sides, with the differential capacitance between the diaphragm and these plates being converted electronically into a signal.

Operation is based upon the fact that capacitance is directly proportional to plate area and absolute permittivity, and is inversely proportional to the distance between the plates. The principle of a central plate moving in this manner between two fixed plates as part of a capacitor circuit can be used in a variety of applications to produce an electrical signal.

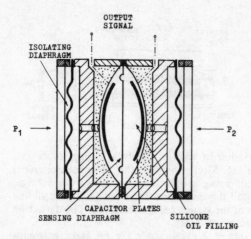

Fig. 69 Variable Capacitance Transducer

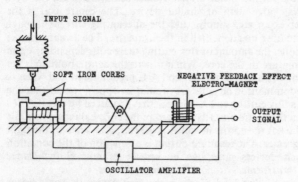

Fig. 70 Force Balance Electronic Transducer

Force Balance Transducer. The basic components of this device are shown in Fig. 70. Here the input, which could be through a bellows, bourdon tube or d.p. cell link, operates a beam about a pivot, changing the air gap between two pieces of soft iron, one attached to the beam, the other fixed. As this gap changes, the inductance of a coil around the fixed piece of soft iron varies. This change of inductance is fed into an oscillator amplifier causing this to vary its output in relation to the change in input, between the limits of 4 to 20mA. This current is then fed to an electro-magnet which produces a negative feedback effect on the beam opposing the input force and bringing about an equilibrium condition.

Electric Telegraph. As shown in Fig. 71 this consists basically of a transmitter consisting of a flat disc of insulating material such as bakelite on which are fixed conductors placed in arcs around the plate. Contact brushes held by a carrier ring and operated by the order transmission lever, bear on these conductors. The receiver has three coils connected as shown with a permanent magnet to which the order pointer is fixed freely rotating between them. Three positions of the telegraph are shown and from these it can be seen that in position 1 two poles of

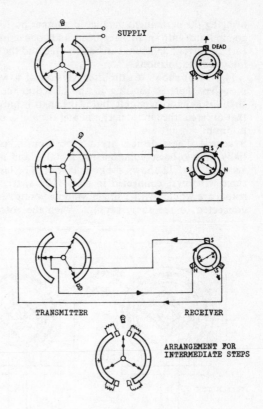

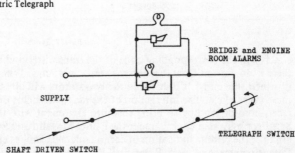

Fig. 71(a)   Electric Telegraph

Fig. 71(b)   Wrong Way Alarm

the receiver are strongly magnetized allowing the permanent magnet to position the pointer to match the transmission lever position. If the latter is moved 30° to 2, one coil is fully magnetized, the current splitting at the other two producing a weaker field in these so that the permanent magnet takes up another position determined by the relative field strengths. If the transmission pointer is moved 150°, it will be seen that the polarity of the two weaker poles has changed, bringing the permanent magnet to another position. By splitting the transmitter commutator into smaller segments and connecting these together by a resistance, further current divisions can be achieved and the receiver can be made to take up intermediate positions.

Fig. 71(b) shows a simplified version of a wrong way alarm switch. If the propeller shaft is rotating in the direction the telegraph indicates the alarm circuit is kept open circuit, but if the shaft is moving in the opposite direction to that ordered, the circuit is closed and the alarm operates. It is shown in the open position.

Synchros. These devices are a.c. position indicating motors, consisting essentially of two basic components, a stator and a rotor, whether transmitter or receiver. Fig. 72 shows a simple layout. The laminated stators are wound with three windings, connected in star, 120° apart. H-shaped laminated iron core rotors are wound with a single winding connected to slip rings, with both rotors connected to the same supply. When the rotor positions coincide, then the

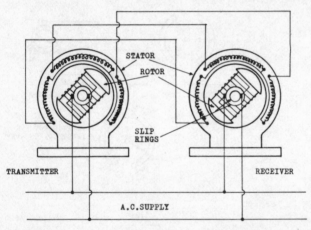

Fig. 72 Synchro

e.m.f.'s in the corresponding coils of the transmitter and receiver are equal, and there is no current flow through the stator windings. When the transmitter rotor is turned, the e.m.f.'s induced in the two stators will alter, and a current flow in these takes place. The interaction of the magnetic fields produces a torque in the receiver rotor tending to bring this into alignment with that of the transmitter. Synchros may also appear under the names Magslip and Selsyn. Such devices are used for the remote indication of cargo tank level gauges etc.

Potentiometer and Self Balancing Bridge. These instruments are used very widely in instrumentation and control circuits to measure a variation in potential difference in part of the circuit caused by a change in the condition being monitored, by balancing this new potential difference against one of known value. A simple basic circuit is shown in Fig. 73(a) in which a change in temperature across a resistance thermometer causes a change in potential difference. By sliding contact 1 along the slide wire resistance, the variation in resistance of the thermometer causing the potential difference between 1 and 2 can be balanced so that the meter then reads zero. In practice, a system based on that

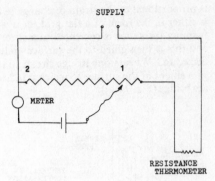

Fig. 73(a)   Potentiometer

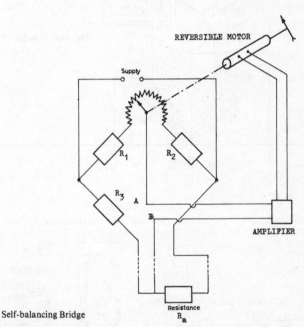

Fig. 73(b)   Self-balancing Bridge

shown in Fig. 73(b) would be used. If the value of resistance Ra changes, the balance of the Wheatstone Bridge is upset and a potential difference is set up between A and B. This is fed to an amplifier which produces a signal relative in value to the change in resistance in Ra, but sufficiently powerful to operate a reversible electric motor. This motor then drives a recorder or indicator and also repositions a slide wire resistance so that the potential difference between A and B is reduced to zero and the bridge is once more in balance.

Resistance Strain Gauge. This type of gauge may be used in two forms with both depending upon the same principle for their operation, namely that a metal wire, when extended or compressed, undergoes a change of electrical resistance which

61

is proportional to the strain or change in length. With the bonded type, the wire is either in the form of a flat grid, or is wound round a helical former. The wire forming the gauge is cemented to a sheet of paper or plastic, or phenolic resin, and this is then glued to the surface under stress. The ends of the wire are connected to a Wheatstone Bridge circuit so that any change in length of wire due to movement of the surface to which it is fixed, alters the resistance and unbalances the bridge (Fig. 74(a)).

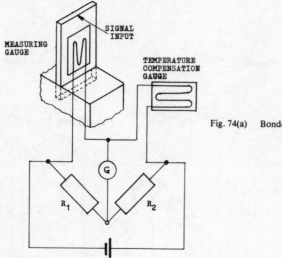

Fig. 74(a)   Bonded Resistance Strain Gauge

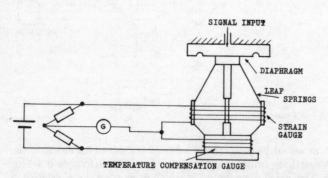

Fig. 74(b)   Unbonded Resistance Strain Gauge

The unbonded type consists of a number of wires wound round support posts in such a way that the posts can be moved and the wires stretched. These wires are also in the form of a Wheatstone Bridge. Fig. 74(b) shows applications. Temperature is an important factor as this can affect the resistance of the wire and cause false readings. Either a wire with a low temperature coefficient of resistivity is used or an unstressed gauge is placed with the stressed gauge, the latter being on the opposite side of the bridge. Wires are about $0 \cdot 01 - 0 \cdot 02$ mm diameter. Metal foil and silicon semi-conductor material, types may also be used.

CHAPTER 7

Automatic Control Theory

This chapter sets out to explain the basic theory involved in the maintenance of an engineering system, such as boiler water level or jacket cooling water temperature of a diesel engine, at a required operating condition without human intervention. The majority of such systems employ automatic closed loop control which may be defined as a system in which, without human intervention, the actual value of a controlled condition, such as level, flow, temperature, viscosity or pressure is compared with a desired (or set) value representing the required operating condition, with corrective action being taken should a deviation or difference occur between these two values.

To fully understand the theory involved it is necessary to use terminology peculiar to this subject, such terminology will, however, be kept to a minimum and is based on the British Standards Publication B.S.1523.

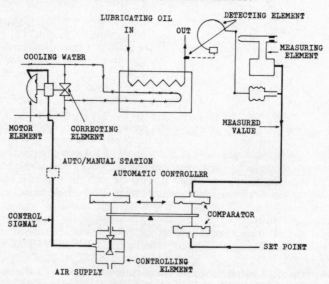

Fig. 75 Closed Loop Control System

Some of the more common terms are listed below and their application to a typical system is shown in Fig. 75. The operation of a plant under automatic control in order to control such variables as temperature, level, flow viscosity etc., is known as *Process Control*. Here the process is the cooling of the lubricating oil in the heat exchanger. Working round the system from the *Process*, the *Controlled Condition* is the temperature of the lubricating oil, and this is monitored by a sensor or *Detecting Element*, which could be a filled systems thermometer connected to a bourdon tube. This operates a noz-zle/flapper device which produces a pneumatic signal, known as the *Measured Value*, whjch is directly related to the temperature of the lubricating oil. The operation of this nozzle/flapper amplifier has been explained previously, and it is known in control engineering terms as a *Measuring Element*, or by some manufacturers as a *Transmitter*. This measured value signal is taken to a *Comparing Element* or *Comparator* forming part of the *Automatic Controller* or *Controlling Unit*. Here it is compared (one method is shown) with a signal representing the required lubricating oil operating temperature or the *Set Value* (*Set Point*) or *Desired Value*. (There could be a difference between these terms which will be explained later in the text). If the *Set Value* and *Measured Value* are the same, the beam will not move, but if there is a difference between these signals, known as the *Deviation*, or *Error*, it means that the lubricating oil temperature at the outlet from the cooler is not at the required operating tem-perature (Set Point etc.,) and action has to be taken to restore it. The difference in signal pressures on the diaphragms will rotate the beam about the pivot, the movement being the *Error Signal* and this will operate the *Controlling Element*.

This develops the signal necessary for the restoration of the oil temperature; the signal may be known as the *Controller Output Signal* or *Control Signal*. This signal is transmitted to the *Motor Element* or diaphragm of a control valve which then operates the *Correcting Element* or valve. This then adjusts the *Correcting Condition* or cooling water flow to enable the oil temperature to be restored.

Feedback is the transmission of a signal representing the controlled condition for comparison with a signal pre-set by the operator, and which is intended to determine the value of the controlled condition. As a loose interpretation Feedback may be considered to be similar to the Measured Value.

Open Loop Control. This means that there is no feedback of information on the value of the controlled condition of, for example, the lubricating oil in Fig. 75, so that the controller has no information on what effect its control of the sea-water valve is having on the oil. This form of control can be used, and has been used, on some accommodation heating systems. Fans pump air across steam heated heat-exchangers, into distribution trunking throughout the ac-commodation. The quantity of steam flowing through the heaters is controlled by a valve, the setting of which is determined by the deck temperature. As long as this temperature remains constant, so will the heat to the air and to the ac-commodation. However, if the air flow changes (or the steam pressure or temperature) then the air could become cooler or hotter, but the steam valve would remain in the same position as it has no feed back of information on the air temperature.

Two Step (on-off) Control. A simple cheap form of control for use on a process where a considerable deviation from the desired value can be tolerated. With such systems a desired value is selected and the automatic controller adjusted so that the correcting unit (a valve, pump or compressor) has only two positions or conditions open/shut, running or stopped. The automatic controller switches the correcting unit from one extreme to the other as the controlled condition passes the set point. In systems such as temperature control of refrigerated domestic store rooms or steam hot water heaters, there is a time lag between the valve operating and the heat passing into the refrigerator and from the steam to the water due to the heat transfer delay by the tube material; this is known as a

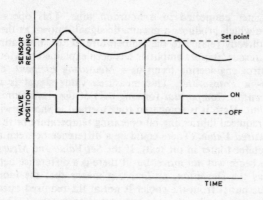

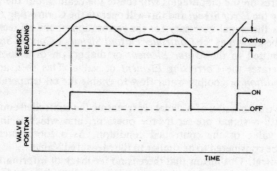

Fig. 76 On-Off Control

Transfer Lag and due to this the store room temperature or water temperature may take time to rise or fall, as in Fig. 76. This tends to prevent oscillation . In systems such as domestic fresh water pressure or level control, the operation of the automatic controller, the valve or pump and associated water flow can be very quick and oscillation can occur. Such systems may be given overlap by the use of limit switches or adjusting the controller. The valve or pump then operates at a pre-set high level or pressure values and at pre-set low values.

Two Step systems are suitable for processes with High Demand Side capacity and a Low Supply Side capacity, i.e., a large capacity hot water tank with a small supply of heat, the reverse would cause oscillation, which can cause rapid wear and tear on components and increased maintenance.

Modulating Control; Continuous Control. These are the names given to control systems which provide a continuous and smooth control action and which can be used to eliminate the oscillation that may occur with two-step control if it is necessary to maintain the controlled condition very close to or at the desired value. The correcting unit, such as a valve, with this form of control can be adjusted to an infinite number of positions between its maximum and minimum limits.

Proportional Control. This is the basic form of modulating control in which the controller is set up so that any change in output is directly proportional to the deviation between the controlled condition and the desired value.

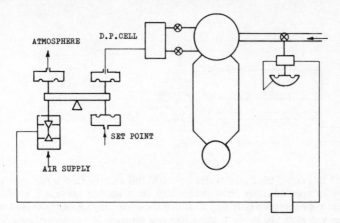

Fig. 77 Proportional Control

Thus, if the level of water in the boiler, in Fig. 77, due to increased steam demand, drops by 20 mm, then the automatic controller output to the feed water inlet valve may change from $0 \cdot 6$ to $0 \cdot 7$ bar. If the level drops by 40 mm, then the automatic controller output would change from $0 \cdot 6$ to $0 \cdot 8$ bar. To obtain optimum performance from a control system and the plant, the former must be capable of adjustment to suit the particular characteristics of the latter. In order to do this, the amount by which the controller output changes for a given alteration in input can be adjusted when the system is first set up, and subsequently, should any changes take place as characteristics alter due to age. The adjustment is made by altering the amplification of the controller, or the number of times the change in the input signal is repeated in the output signal change. The variable amplification is known as the *Proportional Band* of the controller and is measured by the percentage of the input range available that is required to make the output signal change over its full range. Thus, if the input signal (or error signal) to the controller ranges from $0 \cdot 2$ bar to $1 \cdot 0$ bar, and the ouput from the controller ranges from $0 \cdot 2$ bar to $1 \cdot 0$ bar, then the proportional band is 100 per cent i.e. it takes the full input signal range to give the full output signal range. If, however, the input signal only has to change from $0 \cdot 2$ bar to $0 \cdot 6$ bar, i.e., 50 per cent of its range, to make the output change from $0 \cdot 2$ bar to $1 \cdot 0$ bar, then the proportional band is said to be 50 per cent. From these figures it can be seen that the output signal change ($0 \cdot 8$ bar) is twice the input signal (error signal) change ($0 \cdot 4$ bar). Thus the automatic controller has multiplied the input signal change by a factor of 2. This is known as the *Gain* of the automatic controller.

The effect of varying the proportional band or automatic controller output for a set change in error signal or input signal is shown in Fig. 78.

Offset/Droop. When a disturbance occurs to the controlled condition due to a change in plant loading, the correcting unit will have to move to a new position in order to counteract the effect and restore equilibrium, i.e. if the steam demand

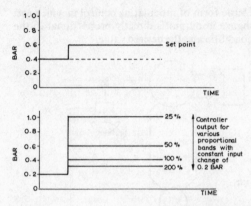

Fig. 78 Effect of Varying Gain

in Fig. 77 increases, the boiler water level will fall and the feed water inlet valve will have to open to allow more water into the boiler to prevent it eventually emptying. However, the only way in which the correcting unit (or the feed water controller valve) can be made to move to a new position in a proportional control system is for an error or deviation to occur, i.e. for the controlled condition (water level) to move away from the desired value. If the feedwater control valve is therefore initially at half stroke and has to move to three-quarters stroke, for the water supply to match the steam demand, then the controller output signal must change by 25 per cent of its range. (If the output range is 0·2 to 1·0 bar, it must change from 0·6 to 0·8 bar, for example).

If the automatic controller has a proportional band setting of 50 per cent (a gain of 2), then the input signal must alter by $12\frac{1}{2}$ per cent (i.e. 0·1 bar) to bring about this output change, and hence the boiler water level must fall. If the boiler water level measuring unit has a range of 0–400 mm, then this change in level means a fall of 50 mm. Once equilibrium has been established, the boiler will operate about a new water level 50 mm below the level existing before the increase in steam demand. For each change in steam demand a new level will exist. The difference between the previous and existing level is known as *Offset* and sometimes as *Steady State* error or *Ultimate State* error. This offset will remain until a new steam demand causes a change.

Desired Value, Set Value (Set Point). Confusion can arise over the use of these terms and they are frequently used to indicate the same value. The set value (set point) represents the value of the controlled condition to which the comparing element is set, and is usually the desired value. When using a proportional controller however, the value of the controlled condition actually obtained in a steady state, (the control point), differs from this desired value as load changes arise, and this difference is known as the offset. To allow for this, the set value may be adjusted to a value which is different from the desired value. If, for example, in the case of the boiler water level previously discussed, it is necessary to maintain a water level of 100 mm in the gauge glass and this is the desired value, then with the load change described, this level drops to 50 mm, and there is an offset of 50 mm. The operator would then be required to re-adjust the set value to 150 mm for the water level to be controlled at the 100 mm desired value condition.

This set point alteration would have to be made with each load change. Such precision of definition is not always used and, in line with most books, set point (value) and desired value will be taken henceforth to be the same.

Offset can be reduced by increasing the gain or sensitivity of the controller. This is achieved by adjusting the proportional band setting, reducing or narrowing the band (a lower percentage reading, higher gain reading) and requiring a smaller variation between the measured value and desired value to give an output signal change over the full signal range.

In the previous case with a 50 per cent proportional band setting, an input signal change of $0 \cdot 1$ bar brought about an output signal change of $0 \cdot 2$ bar. If this proportional band setting is reduced to 25 per cent (gain of 4) it means that only a quarter of the measured value range has to be used to cause the output signal to change over its complete range, or an input signal change of $0 \cdot 05$ bar brings about an output change of $0 \cdot 2$ bar and opens the valve by 25 per cent. Thus if the proportional band is narrowed a very small deviation between the measured value and desired value can cause a very large change in output signal. In the case of the boiler feed water control valve, a small change in level could cause the valve to open to its full position allowing such an inrush of water that the level would be lifted far above the desired value. As the control system tries to correct for this, the valve shuts in and the flow virtually stops. This oscillation or surging effect with rapid opening and closing of the valve is called *hunting* and should be avoided at all costs as it causes damage to the plant and excessive wear and tear on control and plant equipment. The effect of varying the proportional band is shown in Fig. 79.

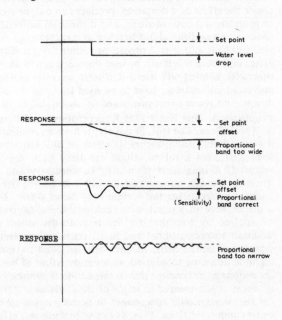

Fig. 79 Hunting

Proportional Plus Reset Control. Two Term Control Proportional Plus Integral Control. The problems of hunting (instability) and offset inherent in the proportional controller can be overcome by using *Integral Action or Reset Action* added to a proportional controller. Thus, if the characteristics of a particular plant are such that, under proportional control, any attempt to reduce the offset by narrowing the proportional band produces hunting, the proportional band has to be kept wide and reset action added to eliminate the offset effect. The addition of reset action causes *the output of the controller* to *change at a rate proportional to the deviation between the set value and the measured value.* In the case of the boiler feed water control valve, if the water level changes, the controller first generates a signal proportional to the deviation, which moves the feed water control valve in proportion to the deviation, so that the inflow of water matches steam outflow. Then the reset action is applied at a rate proportional to the deviation, so that the valve continues to open, the water inflow exceeding the steam demand, thus restoring the level. As the desired value of the water level is approached, the reset action falls away, the valve starts to close down, until at the desired water level, the reset action disappears and the valve is under proportional control, open the required amount so that the steam and water flows are balanced.

An adjustment on the automatic controller allows free variation of the reset or integral action effect. It is usually meaured in minutes of *integral action time,* or *repeats per minute.* The former is defined as *the time taken for the integral action to repeat the proportional action when there is a constant error present.* Repeats per minute measurement is arrived at thus: if the automatic controller, under the effect of a deviation, produces an output signal change of $0 \cdot 2$ bar due to proportional control alone, and if the reset action due to the same deviation, produces an additional $0 \cdot 4$ bar output signal change every minute, then the reset rate will be $0 \cdot 4 / 0 \cdot 2 = 2$ repeats per minute. Figs. 80(a and b) show reset action effect and from this it can be seen that such action should be applied cautiously, otherwise hunting will occur. On start-up, reset action may produce instability and hand control may have to be used to bring the process to the control condition. This is due to the prolonged deviation that exists in this condition.

Proportional Plus Reset Plus Rate (Proportional Plus Integral Plus Derivative) or Three Term Control. Some plants have an inherent characteristic such that when a disturbance occurs, because of the large volumes and/or masses or long distances involved, there are long time delays before equilibrium is restored. A long reset time may be necessary and if there is a tendency to hunting, a wide proportional band will be required. In fact, if the disturbances are frequent, the system may never settle. To improve recovery from a disturbance in a plant with such problems, *Derivative* or *Rate Action* may be applied by adding a further term to the automatic controller output, in addition to proportional and reset. Such action tends to stabilize the control system and allows either the proportional band to be narrowed, or a shorter integral action time to be used, or a combination of both. *With derivative action the output signal change due to this action is proportional to the rate of change of error.* It is measured in terms of the *Derivative Action Time—the time taken for the proportional component to become equal to the derivative component under ramp conditions.* Figs. 81 (a and b) show this effect.

An important point to realize is that the rate of action is dependent upon the rate of change in error, or the rate at which it is developing, and not upon the

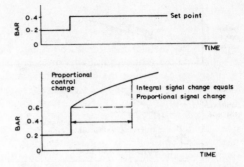

Fig. 80(a)   Integral Action Time

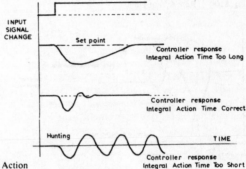

Fig. 80(b)   Effect of Varying Integral Action

amount of error. Thus a considerable corrective action is possible for a small error or deviation if it takes place rapidly. Also, a long derivative action time means that the proportional action takes longer to repeat the derivative action, and assuming the gain or proportional band constant, the derivative action is therefore greater than wtih the shorter derivative action time. This is the reverse to integral action time, where the shorter the time, the greater the effect. Derivative action adjustments should only be made in very small amounts over a long period, for excessive amounts can cause hunting and instability.

Split Range Control. The output signal from a controller may be split into two or more branches to control two or more correcting units. A typical marine application is shown in Fig. 82 where a single temperature sensor, via an automatic controller, controls two valves to maintain the jacket cooling water of a diesel engine constant. The jacket cooling water outlet temperature sensor monitors the cooling water at the outlet from the cylinder head (resistance thermometer, thermocouple or thermistor for electrical control circuits, filled system type for a pneumatic control system and possibly for an electrical system via a transducer), and feeds a signal to the autmoatic controller where the comparing element checks for any deviation. The automatic controller output usually ranges from $0 \cdot 2$ bar to $1 \cdot 0$ bar and this is fed to both valve positioners. These are adjusted so that when the jacket cooling water temperature is low, the low air signal $0 \cdot 2$

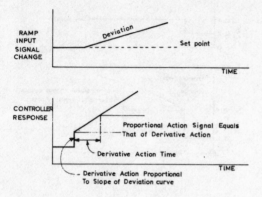

Fig. 81(a)   Rate Action Time

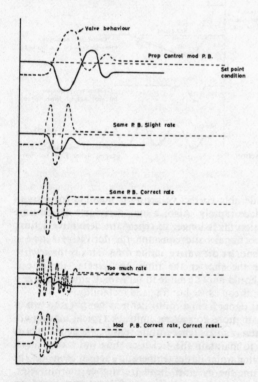

Fig. 81(b)   Effect of Varying Rate Action

bar—0·4 bar operates the steam supply valve to raise the temperature of the water. When the pressure is above 0·4 bar this valve is shut, and the 0·4 bar—1·0 bar range, the cooling water valve, is open. Below 0·4 bar this valve is shut, so that there is only one valve open at any time.

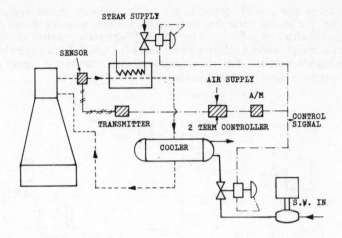

Fig. 82 Split Range Control Application

In some cases where there would be problems with two valves open at one time, a dead band is used, one valve closing at 0·4 bar for instance and the other opening at 0·5 bar. This would be used when using exhaust steam and bled steam for deaerating feed water for boilers. Excess exhaust steam may be dumped to a condenser, but to prevent this happening to steam bled from the turbines, the dead band ensures that the dump valve is shut before the bled steam valve opens. This dead band is not required in the cooling water system.

Ratio Control. This form of control holds the ration between two or more measured variables constant. Probably the most common marine application is in boiler combustion control systems where air flow and fuel flow are maintained in a desired ratio to provide efficient combustion. Usually the air flow is controlled by dampers, vanes or varying fan speed, to match the fuel flow.

Cascade Control. By suitable adjustment of proportional band, integral action time, and possibly rate action time, an automatic control system can deal with the time lag between a deviation arising and equilibrium being restored, introduced by a large capacitor, whether it is a large volume of water or a large thermal storage capacility.

However, when two such capacitors are involved control can become more difficult and it may be necessary to use cascade control. This involves two automatic controllers in series, the output signal of one, the master, being used as the set point of the second, the slave. The output signal from this is then used to adjust the correcting unit. Each automatic controller has a sensor providing a measured value signal of the system under control from a different position in the plant. In this way the two capacitors are split into two single capacitor systems making control easier.

Maintaining a constant cooling water outlet temperature from the cylinder jackets of a diesel engine presents problems due to the thermal inertias of the large mass of water flowing and the engine and coolers, all being thermal capacitors. Variations in engine loading whilst manoeuvring, and in sea water, temperatures and possibly pressure, add to the problem. In this application, therefore, the master controller responds to the sensor at the jacket outlet, compares it with a set point signal introduced by the plant operator and if there is a deviation, produces a resetting signal which is taken to the set point bellows of the slave controller. The slave controller then transmits a signal to the correcting unit (valve) which adjusts the sea water flow. (Fig. 83).

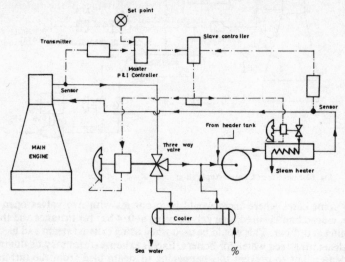

Fig. 83 Cascade Control Application

Thus the effect of any change in engine loading on jacket cooling water outlet temperature is sensed by the master controller which operates the sea water control valve at the cooler via the set point of the slave controller.

If there is a change in sea water temperature or pressure, this will immediately affect the water in the cooler and the outlet temperature here is monitored by a sensor, to which the slave controller responds. Any change in this temperature operates the slave controller which acts as a self-contained control loop to re-adjust the sea water control valve. Thus any temperature change at the cooler due to sea water temperature or pressure fluctuation is prevented from reaching the engine and causing a temperature change in the whole system which would take a long time to sense and correct.

System Response. The ideal control system would instantaneously respond to a deviation and restore the plant to the desired value without any delay, overshoot, hunting etc. Time delays and system lags caused by the behaviour of the various components will delay the response of the control system to a deviation and these have to be catered for in design and when setting the system up. Example of such lags are as follows:-

Distance Velocity Lag. If oil is flowing through a heater and the steam supply is suddenly increased raising the oil temperature, then this temperature increase will not appear at the detecting element or sensor until some time has passed due to the finite rate of flow of the fluid. To reduce such a lag the thermometer should be close to the heater.

74

Measurement Lag. This is the time taken for a measuring unit to assume a new value when a change in the controlled condition of the fluid, gas etc., takes place due to disturbance. When measuring flow with a mercury manometer, if a change in flow takes place, there will be a time delay as the mercury flows from one leg to the other.

Transfer Lag. This is sometimes known as multi-capacity lag and occurs, for example, with the transfer of heat energy to the resistance of the material to heat flow and the time taken to alter the quantity of heat stored in the material, or its thermal inertia.

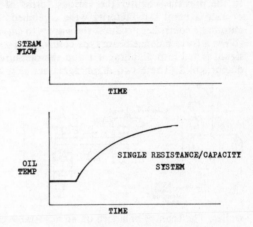

Fig. 84 Resistance/Capacity Lag

The oil heater mentioned previously will have a transfer lag due to the capacity affect of the oil in the heater. If the steam (hence heat) supply is suddenly increased in a step input, as shown in Fig. 84, initially when there is a large temperature difference between the oil and steam, the heat flow is rapid and the oil temperature rises quickly. As the oil temperature rises, the temperature difference between it and the steam drops, the heat flow reduces and the rate of rise decreases, producing the curve shown, known as an exponential curve. The resistance of the tube material to heat flow, and the capacity effect of the heater produce a single resistance capacity lag, or an exponential lag or a first order lag. If the heat storage capacity of the insulation is considered it introduces another capacitor, giving a two capacity lag. The greater the number of such lags the more difficult the control problems are to solve. The oil is termed the demand side thermal capacity or demand lag as it *demands* heat and the steam, the lagging and heater the supply side thermal capacity or supply lag. For good control the smaller the supply side capacity in relation to the demand side, the better the control. A very large heat supply would vary the oil temperature rapidly and cause oscillation or hunting.

CHAPTER 8

Automatic Controllers

In the previous chapter the various forms of automatic control required to operate a plant satisfactorily were explained. This chapter explains how the automatic controller produces the signals to carry out these functions. Fig. 85(a) shows a force balance beam type controller. Here the desired value or set point signal is fed into diaphragm 1 and the measured value signal is fed on to the diaphragm 2. These two diaphragms act as a comparing element of the con-

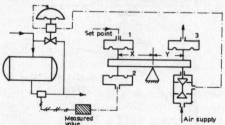

Fig. 85(a)   Proportional Controller

troller. The beam is balanced on an adjustable pivot and operates a relay at the opposite end. For *proportional control* diaphragm 3 is open to atmosphere. Assume that under equilibrium conditions, the pressures on diaphragm 1 and 2 are equal at $0\cdot6$ bar. Consider the control of lubricating oil temperature and a condition of an increased engine loading so that the oil temperature rises. The measured value signal also rises as the sensor or detecting element monitors rise and causes the measuring unit (or transmitter) to increase its output signal, (measured value) in proportion. Let this increase be $0\cdot1$ bar so that the pressure on diaphragm 2 is $0\cdot7$ bar, whilst that on diaphragm 1 is at the desired value at $0\cdot6$ bar, representing the required operating temperature. An error of $0\cdot1$ bar indicates that a deviation has occurred and the inbalance of diaphragm loading causes the beam to rotate clockwise. With the pivot in the middle ($x = 1:y = 1$) the right hand side of the beam moves the same amount as the left hand side, and the relay exhaust valve shuts, the inlet opening so that the output increases by $0\cdot1$ bar.

This is zero again or a 100 per cent proportional band setting as the full range of the measured value signal is required to produce a full range output signal from the controller.

If the pivot is moved towards the right hand side of the beam so that $x = 1\cdot5$ and $y = 0\cdot5$ then for the same temperature change and error of $0\cdot1$ bar, taking moments about the pivot

$$(0\cdot7 - 0\cdot6) \times 1\cdot5 \ = \ \text{Output change} \times 0\cdot5$$

$$\frac{0\cdot1 \times 1\cdot5}{0\cdot5} \ = \ \text{Output change} = 0\cdot3 \text{ bar}$$

Thus by moving the pivot to the right, for the same deviation the gain has been increased (by 3 in this case) and the proportional band narrowed to $33\frac{1}{3}\%$, with the sensitivity increased. Moving the pivot further to the right would increase the gain further, bringing the controller virtually to an ON-OFF condition. Such a move would be likely to promote hunting. In general $(P_2-P_1)x = (P_0-P_3)y$

$$\text{or} \quad P_0 = \frac{(P_2-P_1)x}{y} + P_3$$

P_3 is open to atmosphere and thus is zero as all the pressures involved use atmospheric pressure as datum.

Moving the pivot to the left reduces the gain and widens the proportional band.

As this is a proportional controller, the valve controlling the cooling water flow or the lubricating oil by-pass at the cooler would only move an amount proportional to the error or deviation and depending upon the gain or proportional band setting there would be some degree of offset in the lubricating oil temperature.

Integral Action or **Reset Action** may be applied to eliminate this offset (and to allow the proportional band to be widened to eliminate hunting if this is present due to attempts to reduce the offset), by adding an adjustable resistance valve and a capacitor between diaphragm 3 and the output pressure line as in Fig. 85(b). Assume similar conditions as previously with an increase in lubricating oil temperature causing an increase in controller output pressure. If the proportional band is set for a gain of 3 so that for a deviation signal of 0.1 bar, the output is 0.3 bar. In Fig. 85(b) this output signal is now led to the resistance valve which determines the time taken for the pressure in diaphragm (3) to be affected by any change in the output pressure. As this output pressure increases

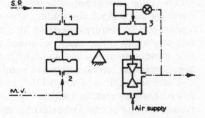

Fig. 85(b)   Proportional + Reset Controller

to 0.3 bar, so the pressure on diaphragm 3 increases, the increasing force tending to move the beam further clockwise about the pivot. This opens the supply valve of the relay further, again increasing the output, which in turn increases the force on diaphragm 3. This integral or reset action continues until the maximum output of 1.0 bar is reached, or until the temperature deviation has been eliminated and the set point and measured value signals are equal.

The effect of this increasing output signal is to open up the sea water on the cooler, or shut in the oil by-pass, beyond the position created by proportional control until the set point temperature has been restored possibly to the limit of its stroke, and then bring it back to a position for equilibrium as the reset action dies away. The time taken to do this depends upon the resistance valve setting. With the valve just cracked open, the time taken for the output pressure to affect diaphragm 3 and adjust the valve beyond the proportional control position would be considerable. With it wide open the time would be short and over-correction and hunting would be likely to occur.

This is an example of positive feed back. The reverse to the above events takes place if there is a fall in lubricating oil temperature.

Derivative or **Rate Action** is achieved by the use of a second controller connected as shown in Fig. 85(c). The measured value is fed to diaphragm 5 without any restriction and also to diaphragm (6) but this time with a restriction orifice and capacitor. Thus any increase in measured value due to, for example, an increase in lubricating oil temperature, causes an immediate increase in pressure on diaphragm 5 but the change in pressure on diaphragm 6 depends upon the amount the restriction valve is open. If it is wide open then the force on the two

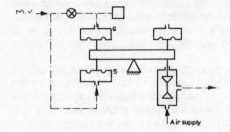

Fig. 85(c)   Addition for Rate Control

diaphragms cancel each other and there is no rate action. If it is just cracked open, the initial force difference between the two diaphragms is large and the beam would move rapidly in a clockwise direction, giving a very large increase in the output signal. As the pressure builds up on diaphragm 6 so a restoring force slowly comes into action. The effect of the two term controller will also tend to move the beam clockwise adding its own output signal to that of the rate action. The reverse procedure happens with a decrease in lubricating oil temperature. In this way a quick response is obtained to a deviation to overcome time lags and give rapid correction, but again with the rate restriction valve shut in too far, over correction can result, to give hunting.

A rate action time of about 1/5th to 1/8th of the integral action time is a guide to assist adjustment, but adjustments should be made in small amounts and the system behaviour checked carefully. Note that to increase rest or integral action the restriction valve is opened, whilst to increase rate action the valve is shut in. Adjustment of the pivot will also affect the immediate rate behaviour. Although rate can be added to proportional control without reset action, most marine controllers are two term, with the third term added in special cases of long plant time delays.

Fig. 86 shows a three term controller employing a nozzle/flapper and relay valve to generate a signal. The set point can be adjusted remotely by using a bellows to set the nozzle/flapper gap to give the required operating condition. The input signal (pressure, temperature transducer etc.) adjusts the flapper about the fixed pivot provided by the set point bellows, varying the air flow to the relay valve and hence the output pressure. Proportional band adjustment is provided by moving the pivot between the levers—when at the top the feedback is reduced, when at the bottom it is increased. Negative feedback (feedback that moves the flapper back towards its original position) is provided by bellows B_1

with the valve 'D' wide open and valve 'I' shut. This is then a proportional controller. As valve 'I' is opened, so any change in output signal pressure affects bellows B_2 and opposes the feedback bellows B_1 movement.

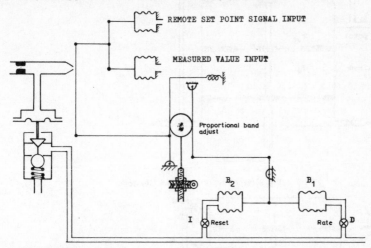

Fig. 86 Nozzle/Flapper Controller

This reset action depends upon the setting of restriction valve 'I' when it is cracked open, the pressure change in bellows B_2 is over a long period and the opposition to bellows B_1 takes time to build up giving a weak integral action effect. If valve 'I' is wide open the pressure change in bellow B_2 is immediate, as it is in bellows B_1 and there is no feedback. This gives a strong reset action.

For rate action a restrictor valve is placed in the line to bellows B_1. As this valve 'D' is *shut in*, the air flow to bellows B_1 is restricted when an output signal change takes place and this delays the provision of negative feedback to the flapper so that it tends to stay in the initial position produced by the movement of the input bellows. The position taken up and the time taken to move the flapper depends upon the relative settings of valves 'I' and 'D', but in the extreme, with 'D' shut and 'I' wide open, the flapper would move even further in the direction of the initial movement given by the input bellows (i.e., if the input signal reduces the gap, then the above condition would reduce it further).

A Stacked Type Controller is shown in Fig. 87(a). The diaphragms are of a material such as Neoprene and the smaller cones are usually half the area of the larger. The set point and measured value signals are applied as shown and proportional band or gain adjustment is achieved by the adjustable restrictor Rg which varies the feedback from the output to the space above the upper diaphragm. The pressure in this chamber is determined by the setting of this valve and the restrictor Y in a line from a constant pressure source, in this case the set point. In some designs it is taken from the supply. Under equilibrium conditions, Forces up = Forces down.

$$P \times A + P_{sp}(A-a) = P_1 \times A + P_{mv}(A-a)$$
$$(P-P_1)A = (P_{mv}-P_{sp})(A-a)$$

and under no error conditions $P_{mv} = P_{sp}$ and $P = P_1$.

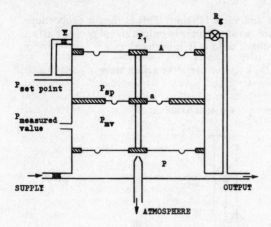

Fig. 87(a)   Proportional Stack Controller

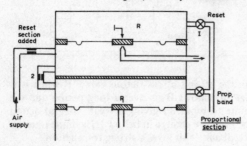

Fig. 87(b)   Proportional + Reset Stack Controller

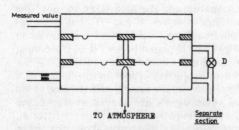

Fig. 87(c)   Rate Controller addition

If the measured value signal rises (P_{mv} increases) for example, due to the difference in diaphragm areas, the control column moves down restricting the flow of air through the nozzle to atmosphere so that the output pressure P increases. P is also negative feedback acting to lift the diaphragm in opposition to the original movement. This pressure is then fed back to the upper chamber through R_G (provided this is open) so that P_1 increases. The resultant output pressure is then $P = (P_{mv}-P_{sp}) (A-a)/A +$ increase in P_1. This is positive feedback.

Fig. 87(b) shows a proportional + reset stack relay. A change in the measured value will cause the central rod to move and adjust the output signal as described above. This signal is now fed back to chamber R via adjustable restriction valve 'I' where it adjusts a second nozzle/flapper created by diaphragm 1. This varies the pressure in the chamber beneath by adjusting the air flow to atmosphere. Through the restriction (2) the pressure in chamber P_1 is altered causing further re-adjustment of the central rod and the cycle of events starts again with the central rod continuously altering the output as long as an error exists.

Fig. 83(c) shows a derivative or rate action unit which would have to be added to the above to give a three term controller. Here an increasing measured value signal restricts the air escape to atmosphere by closing in the exhaust and via adjustable restriction D passes air back to the middle chamber to try to achieve equilibrium. The pressure from the lower chamber is passed to the measured value chamber in the stack relay. By adjusting 'I' and 'D' in both relays the response can be made to suit plant requirements as in the previous types.

Electronic Controller. The basic approach is similar to that of the pneumatic types, a set point signal being compared with the measured value signal and any deviation detected being used to operate the automatic controller. This then produces a restoring signal to the correcting unit proportional band adjustment, reset and rate action are applied in the controller feedback circuit as with pneumatic types, by adjusting variable resistors and the use of capacitors. The set point usually takes the form of a variable resistance, with the current flow through it in the range 0–10 mA or similar values. The sensor signal may be suitable for direct use or may be amplified or converted in a transducer to a suitable scale for comparison purposes.

The operator sets the set point current to suit the required operating conditions of the process under control. Any deviation between this signal and the measured value signal is detected by passing two currents in opposition through a common resistor, the voltage across this then being proportional to the error. This signal is then amplified, and here every effort has to be taken to ensure that during the amplification it still remains true in relation to the actual error and does not 'drift' off value. This is particularly important when there is zero error, for if the amplifier drifts and produces a signal, the control circuit will start correcting for a deviation that doesn't exist. D.c. amplifiers tend to drift and so the error signal is converted to a.c. where zero drift is less of a problem. This conversion is achieved by energizing transistors with an a.c. signal and making them operate as ON-OFF switches, chopping the d.c. signal. Such an amplifier has a virtually zero output with zero input signal. The amplified signal is then rectified to d.c. for use for control purposes.

To obtain proportional band or gain control and to provide reset and rate action, a feedback circuit is incorporated. The output signal is fed back into the input circuit of the amplifier, after having been suitably amplified in the feedback circuit, so that the signals match, and connected to give negative feedback (oppose the error signal).

By adjusting the setting of the proportional band resistor, a change is produced in the relative value of the voltage feed back. This modifies the amplifier input so that the amplifier gain is varied in proportion to the error.

The reset action time is varied by adjusting the variable resistance R_1 which with the capacitor C_1 delays the feedback of the voltage signal to the error signal amplifier, so that the gain is kept high. Fig. 88(a) shows the basic diagram of an electronic two term controller and Fig. 88(b) that of a three term controller. The derivative effect is achieved by the time it takes to charge the derivative capacitor and hence adjust the derivative time of the controller.

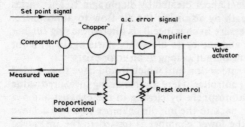

Fig. 88(a)   Electronic Proportional + Reset Controller

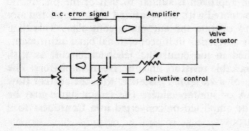

Fig. 88(b)   Electronic Three term Controller

Pulse Controller. In the conventional control systems featured so far, the controller generates an output signal continuously in order to position a valve, for example, and then once the valve position is set, it must maintain a fixed output to hold it there. The pulse controller only transmits a signal to the valve actuator when it needs to be moved and in the absence of a signal the actuator stays where last placed indefinitely.

As Fig. 89 shows, a step change in set value signal produces a long constant amplitude pulse followed by a number of narrow pulses of the same amplitude, with the valve moving at constant velocity for the length of each pulse. The controller, instead of varying over a standard signal range has only three separate outputs—raise, lower and zero and as the actuator only responds to raise or lower demand signals, when there is no signal it holds its previous position. This behaviour allows instantaneous 'bumpless' transfer from Auto to Hand and vice-versa and also a 'fail safe in the last position' feature. Two term control can be provided.

Controller Adjustments. The following is offered as a general guide towards setting up the various forms of controller, but the manufacturers handbook instructions should be given preference, if available.

In all cases the first step is to put the system into manual control and adjust so that the measured value and desired value are the same.

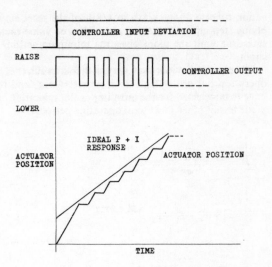

Fig. 89 Pulse Controller

For proportional control only, set the proportional band to the widest value, switch to automatic control according to makers instructions, and then step up or down the set point value and watch the plant response. Return to the original set point and halve the proportional band, then step the set point again to assess plant response. Repeat this procedure, returning to set point etc., until the plant oscillates for 1·5 cycles before settling. This is then the optimum proportional band and is sometimes called quarter amplitude damping.

For a two term controller, after carrying out the first step set the proportional band to 100 per cent and open the reset action valve momentarily, then close it and follow by switching to automatic control under makers instructions. There should be no offset. Step the set point up or down a small amount, sufficient to get a plant response and repeat the procedure for proportional control adjustment until the plant produces *four* cycles before settling, this is the Critical Proportional Band. Measure the time for one oscillation under this condition and then double the proportional band, put in a step change as previously and see whether plant settles in 1·5 oscillations (If not make slight adjustments until this condition is achieved). Set the integral (reset) action time to that taken previously for one oscillation, this is the periodic time of the plant, and then keep applying step adjustments and watching plant response, returning to the original set point each time, whilst adjusting the reset action time until the plant makes around two cycles before settling.

To set up a three term controller, carry out the first step as previously, set proportional band to 100 per cent, open both reset and rate action valves, shutting the former after about a minute. Switch to automatic control as per makers instructions and proceed as for the two term controller until the critical proportional band is found, measuring the periodic time at this condition. Double the proportional band, checking and adjusting for optimum condition as described previously. Set the reset action time at plant period time and adjust around this setting until the plant settles after about 2 oscillations. Set the rate action time to about 1/5th to 1/8th of the reset action time and then keep applying step inputs, returning to the desired value each time, whilst adjusting the rate time until the plant gives the minimum settling time and minimum overshoot.

The plant behaviour may vary with load, such that hunting occurs on low load operation but not at high load, or vice-versa, and the best plant response will have to be selected for the most important operating condition, with adjustments made to suit other short term operating periods.

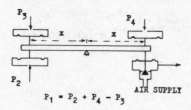

$$P_1 = P_2 + P_4 - P_3$$

Fig. 90(a)   Adding and Subtracting Relay

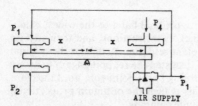

Fig. 90(b)   Averaging Relay

Relays. These can be used for a variety of purposes such as adding, subtracting and averaging, and the connections for these are shown in Fig. 90.

Fig. 91(a) shows a means of remote adjustment of set point by generation of a pneumatic signal. This could also be used for remote operation of a valve etc.

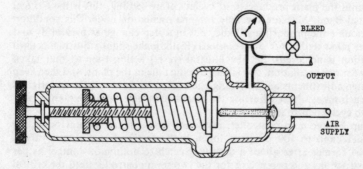

Fig. 91(a)   Remote Set Point Adjustment

The output signal pressure acting on the diaphragm produces a force equal to the spring force set up by the hand control knob. Changing the spring pressure enables the operator to change the output signal. The basic operation of this switch consists of a bellows which expands and contracts as the process condition being monitored (e.g. pressure or temperature) changes. This bellows movement operates the pivoted beam and is counterbalanced by the main spring pressure. When a pre-set spring pressure is exceeded by the bellows pressure the pivot arm moves and opens or closes the contacts. To prevent arcing at the contacts and to ensure a clean, sharp make or break in the power supply of the device being operated a differential spring is built in. If the bellows contract

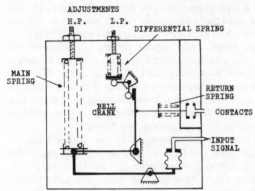

Fig. 91(b)   On-Off Electrical Switch

due to a drop in pressure or temperature of the monitored process, the main spring extends, and at the pre-set switch condition the differential spring lever contacts the main bell crank. The main spring and differential spring are now in opposition, the latter tending to oppose the bellows movement and thus causing the bellows to contract at a slower rate. After the switch has operated the pressure or temperature of the process starts to rise, and the bellows now expands quickly, assisted by the differential spring, but opposed by the main spring. Just before the pre-set high pressure switch point is reached, the differential spring disengages from the bell-crank lever and no longer assists the bellows so that the bellows movement slows down, being opposed by the main spring and without help from the differential spring. The main spring now controls the upper cut out pressure and the differential spring controls the lower pressure.

CHAPTER 9

Supply Systems

Instrument Air. By this is meant an air supply for the instrumentation equipment on the ship and thus requiring a high degree of solid particle filtration, oil and water removal. The presence of solid particles greater than 5 microns in size can cause blockage of orifices, nozzles, and damage to diaphragms and 'O' rings.

Oil may be found in droplet, gaseous and vapour forms, but whatever the form it can create problems by blocking orifices and nozzles, clogging up dryers and building up layers in the pipe lines, eventually blocking them. Moisture present in the air can cause blockage of orifices and nozzles if in droplet form, and cause corrosion, the products of which may cause blockages, and under low temperature conditions, such as a sudden pressure drop, or in low ambient temperatures, it can freeze in the pipe lines or actuator mechanisms.

Fig. 92 shows an air supply system recommended by the BSRA Code of Procedure for Marine Instrumentation and Control Equipment. This particular diagram shows two compressors, but where there is an alternative air supply, as on a motorship, one compressor could be dispensed with. The compressors should preferably be oil of an oil free design, and may be reciprocating non-lubricated water cooled, reciprocating carbon or Teflon ring oil free air cooled, rotary water cooled (requires an efficient air dryer), or rotary oil cooled (requires a large oil separator returning oil to the sump). Water cooled designs may not need after coolers; air cooled designs may need extra coolers and dryers. The supply pressure should be at 7 bar.

As drying and filtering air is expensive, control air for actuators without positioners and general service air may not require to have to be treated to such a high degree as instrument air. However, the water content of the control air will depend upon the application and may have to be dried for use on deck, in cargo holds and refrigerated spaces.

Air Drying. This is usually carried out by refrigeration (using chilled water or brine) by adsorption driers, or by a combination of both, the former being capable of removing about 96 per cent of the moisture and a proportion of the lubricating oil carry area if present.

Adsorption dryers depend upon the condensation of water vapour on the surface of a solid dessicant such as silica gel, activated alumina and synthetic zealite. The water capacity of these is low, but rate of adsorption high, however, high air inlet temperatures reduce the adsorption efficiency of the dessicant, and thus the air must be as cool as possible for maximum moisture removal. Inlet and outlet filters should be provided at the drier, the former to prevent oil clogging the dessicant, the latter to remove dessicant dust which could collect in pipe lines and instrumentation. In the design shown in Fig. 93 twin dryers allow continuous drying to be carried out, one drying air, the other being reactivated. Air enters through a four way valve and passes through the dryer, the dry air then being discharged through a similar valve. At the inlet a small quantity of air

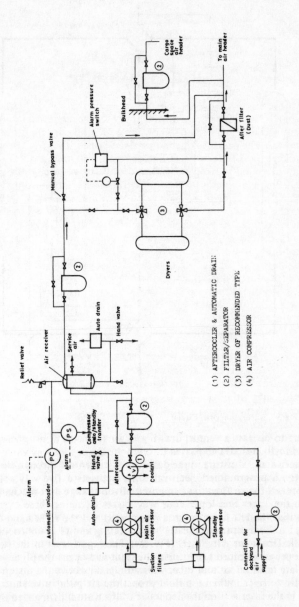

Fig. 92 Control and Instrument Air System

(1) AFTERCOOLER & AUTOMATIC DRAIN
(2) FILTER/SEPARATOR
(3) DRYER OF RECOMMENDED TYPE
(4) AIR COMPRESSOR

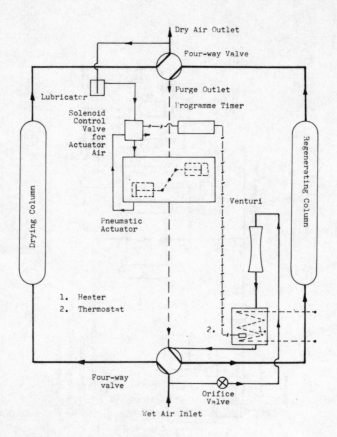

Fig. 93 Adsorption Drier Circuit

is bled off to operate a venturi drawing in air from the atmosphere, and this is then electrically heated and passed through the lower four way valve to the dryer being reactivated. Moisture in the dessicant is driven off through the upper four way valve. A programmed electrical timer actuates a five way solenoid valve which controls the air flow to an opposed piston change over mechanism. This is linked to the upper and lower four way valves changing these over every four hours so that the left hand dryer is reactivated and the right hand dries the instrument air. Regeneration takes $2\frac{1}{2}$ hours heating and $1\frac{1}{4}$ hours cooling.

Automatic Drain for Air Filter. (Fig. 94) The liquid level in the bowl, when it reaches a pre-determined height, lifts the float and opens the pivot valve formed by the plate in the float and tube. This admits air above the piston causing the drain valve to open. When the float drops, the air pilot valve shuts and the air pressure in the filter acts on the underside of the piston, lifting it to shut the drain valve.

Auto-Unloader. (Fig. 95) Used on air compressors, to remove the load when stopping or starting or to act as a relief valve when continuously running and maximum pressure has been reached. This unloader vents the first stage in-

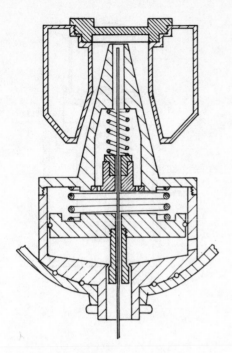

Fig. 94 Automatic Drain

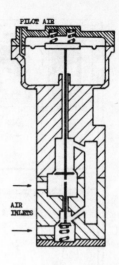

Fig. 95   Auto-Unloader

tercooler and the aftercooler to atmosphere via the compressor's inlet filter silencer, the initial blast of air from the coolers helping to keep the filter clean. If the machine runs for a long period, re-circulation of the air can take place but this is not detrimental as, due to the reciprocating action of the first stage piston, the air demand is fluctuating and hence air continually enters and leaves the filter. The coolers remain effective as the heat dissipation is very small compared with normal conditions.

In operation the unloader is always in the unloaded position, unless air is on the diaphragm, normally from the first stage, overcoming the actuating spring thrust. The pilot air is vented when the maximum pressure required is reached in the compressed air line and the diaphragm springs open the valves. Fig. 96 shows an *air line filter* in which the incoming air passes first through a fine mesh and then ports give it a swirling motion so that centrifugal force flings any water droplets to the casing where it runs into the lower bowl. This may contain an absorption filter.

Fig. 97 shows a *filter regulator* in which the incoming air passes through a mesh filter and then passes up through a regulating valve. The outlet pressure acts on a diaphragm and is counter balanced by an adjustable spring.

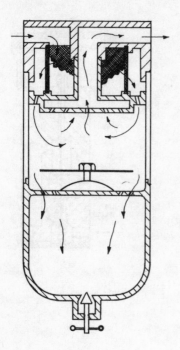

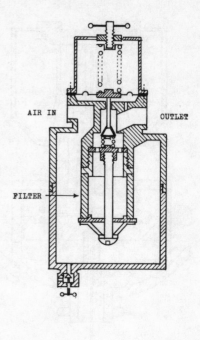

AIR IN   OUTLET

FILTER →

Fig. 96 Air Line Filter   Fig. 97 Filter Regulator

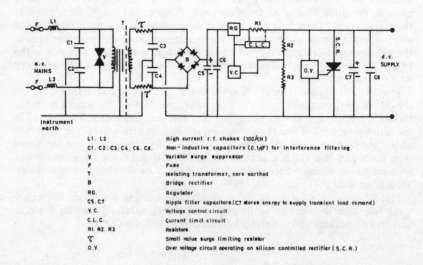

L1. L2	High current r.f. chokes (100μH)
C1. C2. C3. C4. C6. C8.	Non-inductive capacitors (0.1μF) for interference filtering
V	Varistor surge suppressor
F	Fuse
T	Isolating transformer, core earthed
B	Bridge rectifier
RG.	Regulator
C5. C7	Ripple filter capacitors (C7 stores energy to supply transient load demand)
V.C.	Voltage control circuit
C.L.C.	Current limit circuit
R1. R2. R3	Resistors
τ	Small value surge limiting resistor
O.V.	Over voltage circuit operating on silicon controlled rectifier (S.C.R.)

Fig. 98 Supply System for Electronic Circuit

ELECTRICAL SYSTEMS

Electrical interference in electronic systems has to be supressed as far as possible as it can generate spurious signals causing partial or complete loss of data, loss of acuracy, loss of useful signals and the failure of solid state components. It can be generated internally, or capacitvely and inductively coupled into mains or signal leads from other sources. Filtering of a.c. and d.c. lines must take place where they enter the equipment cabinet, which must be totally shielded. Fig. 98 shows circuitry for instrumentation power supply with protection circuits and interference filtering by BSRA.

Signal transmission circuits upon which the operational reliability of electronic control, surveillance and monitoring installations depend may have to transmit data in the presence of large electrical interference signals. Where voltage analogue (d.c. and a.c.) signals are employed, screened cabling must be used to prevent degradation of the transmitted data. Frequency analogue and digital voltage signals can also be degraded by interference, but the information is not greatly affected as it is obtained by counting pulses or frequency periods over a standard time period. Light screening or no screening is feasible here, the latter if interference is light.

With d.c. current transmission the sensor transmitters act as current generators supplying current signals to the equipment low-resistance input circuits. Interference voltages thus have little effect on current signals as these voltages cannot generate significant noise in low resistance input circuits.

CHAPTER 10

Control Valves

The most common means of operating a control valve is pneumatically employing air pressure on a diaphragm, counterbalanced by a spring force. The general arrangement is shown in Fig. 99(a). An air pressure signal from the automatic controller is applied to the topside of the diaphragm, with an increasing air signal pressure pushing the diaphragm plate and spindle down against the force exerted by the spring on the plate. With the valve shown the

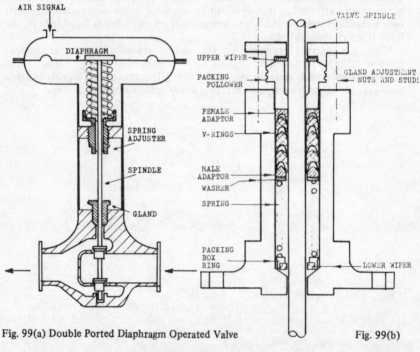

Fig. 99(a) Double Ported Diaphragm Operated Valve   Fig. 99(b)

flow passing through will decrease. The diaphragm/spring unit is called the *motor element* or *actuator*, whilst the valve is called the correcting element. When the air pressure is reduced, the spring forces the valve stem upwards, thus opening the valve. This is called a direct-acting valve or air-to-close (ATC). In theory for every value of air pressure on the diaphragm, whether the valve is opening or closing, there is a particular position for the valve, but valve stem friction in the gland and fluid pressure drop caused by the change in direction of the fluid flow through the valve tend to prevent this ideal behaviour.

The air pressure range on the diaphragm is normally $0 \cdot 2$ to $1 \cdot 0$ bar, although higher pressures can be used and the travel is usually about 90 mm maximum, otherwise non-linearities occur in spring and diaphragm behaviour.

The design can be arranged so that air is supplied on the underside of the diaphragm, using a special seal between the valve stem and diaphragm case so that increasing air pressure on the diaphragm moves the actuator stem upward, whilst loss of air pressure moves the stem downward. This is then known as reverse acting or air-to-open, since the valve opens as the air pressure increases. In some designs instead of changing over the air supply to the underside of the diaphragm, the valve body can be disconnected from the yoke and the actuator stem, the bottom flange taken off and then the complete body inverted and re-connected. As air pressure increases on the top side of the diaphragm, the valve now opens. This is still direct acting, but has the air-to-open (ATO) feature. This is of importance should the air supply to the valve or control system fail, the spring will then cause the valve to shut or open depending upon whether it is ATO or ATC respectively. This feature is also known as fail safe shut, or fail safe open, the spring providing the fail safe force to shut or open the valve. The choice will depend upon the requirements of the system. It is possible by the use of locking valves to lock the valve in a fixed position if air supplies fail. Air is then trapped in the diaphragm giving 'fail safe as is'. There is a requirement that valves must have a means of hand control or a hand operated by-pass. Usually a hand jack is fitted either operating on the diaphragm centre against the spring or on a direct side linkage onto the spindle. This is to provide a means of control should there be a complete failure of air supplies.

The diaphragm case would be of steel, zinc plated, or high tensile iron, the yoke of high tensile iron and the actuator stem of steel, chrome or cadmium plated.

The gland seal or stuffing box is probably the one component that suffers the most operation abuse. It can be responsible for a heavy friction load on the actuator, giving poor positioning control and thus poor plant response. Depending upon manufacturer or application the valve may have a packing requiring lubrication, or self-lubricating packing. In the case of the former, when graphited asbestos or a metallic packing is used, a lantern ring is fitted in way of the lubricator and it is essential that the correct number of packing rings are placed beneath the end above the lantern ring to bring these two components in line. To improve lubrication where temperature permits, Teflon impregnated asbestos may be used. The upper temperature limit here is 230°C, whilst with metallic packing the upper limit is about 480°C.

Moulded Teflon 'V' ring packing or a similar PTFE material can also be used up to 230°C and does not require lubrication, although it may be supplied. Here the stem is highly polished to make use of this type of material whose soapy texture minimizes friction, but it is essential that the 'V' shape is placed so that the pressure of the fluid in the valve expands the 'V' to seal against the side of the gland box and the stem. The gland adjustment is screwed down in this design. A spring, which must be placed in the bottom of the box before the packing is inserted controls the gland pressure. See Fig. 99(b).

On the asbestos adjustable type of gland care must be taken not to screw the gland down too hard, and all old packing must be removed as it is likely to score the spindle. For high temperature operation the gland may have cooling fins around it and for low temperature, cryogenic applications, an extension between

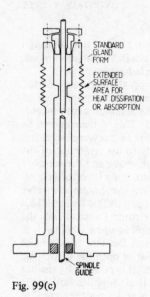

STANDARD
GLAND
FORM

EXTENDED
SURFACE
AREA FOR
HEAT DISSIPATION
OR ABSORPTION

SPINDLE
GUIDE

Fig. 99(c)

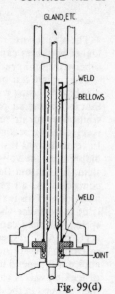

GLAND, ETC.

WELD

BELLOWS

WELD

JOINT

Fig. 99(d)

the valve body and gland may be used to keep the packing at a reasonable temperature (Fig. 99(c)). For hazardous fluids, e.g. explosives or toxic, a bellows seal as Fig. 99(d) can be used, and depending upon pressure they are suitable for temperatures up to 540°C. Great care should be taken of the valve spindle to prevent damage, particularly from overtightening of glands. A felt or PTFE wiper ring is very often used to prevent ingress of dirt to packing boxes.

The control valve or correcting element for most control purposes is a globe valve, with the flow controlled by a specially shaped or characterized valve or plug fitting into a shaped seat. As the fluid has to change direction twice in passing through a single ported valve (Fig. 100(a)) there is a considerable pressure drop which limits the application of this type of valve. This large pressure drop causes considerable out-of-balance forces when flows are large under high pressure conditions, making control difficult and possibly requiring a large diaphragm or high air pressure in the actuator to achieve accurate positioning. They do have the advantage of a tight shut-off, however, and would be used where this is important. In general their application is on small, low flow, low pressure drop applications. They should be fitted with the inflow on the underside of the valve, otherwise when closing, the large pressure drop caused by the inflow on top of the valve will slam it shut.

To overcome these problems a double ported valve is used (Fig. 100(b)) in which the flow passes across two valves (the lower slightly smaller diameter than the upper to allow fitting) in such a way that the out-of-balance forces are nearly balanced out. The size of the actuator can therefore be smaller but the more complex path brings increased flow resistance. It is also more difficult to obtain tight shut off even if the seats are lapped in, as a change in temperature will cause unequal expansion allowing leakage. If the leakage has to be less than 2 per cent of the maximum flow rate, a single ported valve should be used. Even this may not achieve a tight closure unless a soft-seat such as Teflon, or specially designed valves, are used.

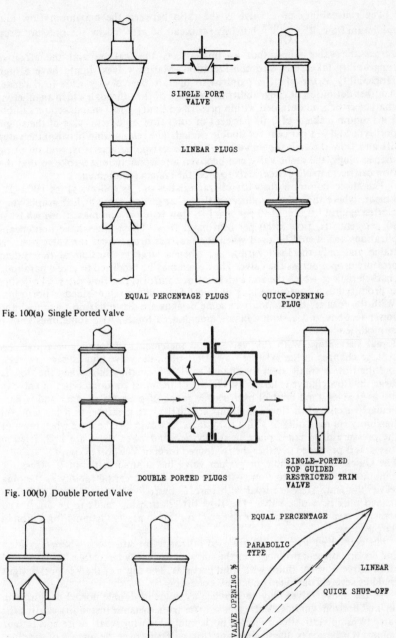

SINGLE PORT
VALVE

LINEAR PLUGS

EQUAL PERCENTAGE PLUGS

QUICK-OPENING
PLUG

Fig. 100(a) Single Ported Valve

DOUBLE PORTED PLUGS

SINGLE-PORTED
TOP GUIDED
RESTRICTED TRIM
VALVE

Fig. 100(b) Double Ported Valve

Fig. 100(c) Parabolic Valve Plugs

EQUAL PERCENTAGE

PARABOLIC
TYPE

LINEAR

QUICK SHUT-OFF

VALVE OPENING %

FLOW AT CONSTANT PRESSURE DROP %

Fig. 100(d) Valve Characteristics

The rangeability of a valve is the ratio between the maximum flow and minimum flow, $R = \dfrac{Qmax}{Qleak}$ but this ratio can be affected by the pressure drop across the valve when shut as this affects the leakage and the effective rangeability takes this into consideration. Marine valves should have a high rangeability as the plant is required to operate over a very wide load range. Another definition of rangeability is the range of flow through which an inherent characteristic is maintained within prescribed limits. Most manufacturers quote a maximum leakage of 0·05 per cent of total flow on a new valve of the single port type and 0·5 per cent for double ported. The relationship between the valve lift and flow through the valve is called the valve characteristic, and by using shaped plugs, the globe valve can be given a reasonably long stroke so that the flow can be controlled accurately to meet the system requirements.

The three common flow-lift characteristics are as follows (Figs 100a–d). **Linear,** where the valve produces a flow that gives a straight line graph when plotted against lift, i.e. at 40 per cent lift, flow is 40 per cent max. flow, whilst at 80 per cent lift, flow is 80 per cent max. flow. These plugs have limited applications and would be used when the pressure drop across the valve remains stable and only the load varies, i.e. when a large proportion of the system pressure drop is across the valve. The design may be modified to give a parabolic characteristic in which the valve gives a fine control at low flow rates. The design is produced as a contoured plug or in the form of a straight sided V-port plug. With the former, the contours in some designs are dissimilar on the upper and lower sections to deal with dynamic unbalanced forces. Also sometimes known as modified linear.

Equal Percentage With this valve equal increments of travel give equal percentage changes in the existing flow, thus when the valve plug is near the seat, and the flow is small, then the change in flow is small, whilst when the flow is large the flow change is large. This is one of the most common types of valve in use as it gives good control over a wide range of pressure changes and is particularly useful when flow conditions are difficult to measure, as it has a useful flexibility for matching or sizing to systems. It would also be used when most of the pressure drop takes place in the system and when there are high friction losses. It is produced in either the contoured form or Vee port (V-pup).

The Quick Opening valve or poppet valve has a small lift, but it offers the minimum obstruction to flow, with the port area increasing rapidly as the plug leaves the seat. They are used with on-off controllers and may have a slightly shaped plug or a disc valve. The flow lift relationship tends to be linear and some, by means of shaping, are designed for this to prevent hammering action in the pipe lines.

The contoured shape plugs are used primarily for situations where corrosion and erosion present problems, as the surfaces can easily be surface hardened and allow a free flow for fluids with solid particles. The edges of the Vee port designs could be severely damaged under this condition.

All the above valves may be supplied as single or double ported design, with top and botttom guiding. Valves may suffer from dynamic instability causing the valve to jump vertically or vibrate horizontally, causing wear, noise and fatigue failure. It is basically due to changing flow patterns, over the surface of the plug, turbulence at the inlet due to the flow impinging on the plug, pressure drop and valve configuration. A hydraulic snubber may be used to reduce the effect or high air pressures and stronger springs or reversing the valve body in the line.

Some valve bodies can be adapted for low flow rates retaining the standard size valve body but using smaller valves and seats. These are known as restricted trim valves and may be contoured, Vee ported or fluted (Fig. 100(b)). The capacity of the valve using this trim style is usually about 40 per cent that of the full body size. Such designs are used when it is not economical to reduce pipe line size to fit a smaller valve and with certain vapour liquid conditions.

The valve body may be of cast iron (−29°C to 350°C), carbon steel (450°C), stainless steel (corrosion resistant) (−100°C to 560°C) chrome molybdenum steel 620°C) or nickel steel (−100°C). The chromium molybdenum steel would have good creep resistance, and some corrosion resistance valve trim can mean the plug seatings, guide bushings, valve stem and internal stuffing box parts and various types of stainless steel or specialized coatings may be used in their manufacture. Extremely erosive conditions may require tungsten carbide, ceramic and urethane elastomers.

The choice of material will depend upon temperature, the lubricating properties of the fluid or gas and the compatibility of the materials to prevent galling or sticking and tearing of mating surfaces. Chromium plating or cobalt based alloys can be used for a solution to this problem. For very low temperature −200°C to +525°C Hastelloy and some chromium plated stainless steels may be used.

Valve Positioners. It may be found when using the signal direct from the controller to the valve diaphragm that when there is a single ported valve in use with a high pressure drop, if the gland has to be tight to deal with a high fluid pressure, if viscous fluids are being dealt with, or if .the valve is a considerable distance from the controller, that the valve will not always be positioned each time it moves at exactly the position in its stroke dictated by the pressure; i.e. at 0·6 bar, when opening it could be at a different position to that at 0·6 bar when closing, as in Fig. 101(a). To overcome this problem a valve positioner is used.

Fig. 101(b) shows such a positioner in which the signal from the controller acting on the bellows is balanced by the force exerted by the positioning spring. If the output signal from the controller increases in value, the bellows will expand and the pilot beam pivots in a clockwise direction, lifting the pilot valve assembly so that air is admitted to the diaphragm acting on the valve spindle. Under the increase in pressure, the valve spindle will move down and operate the drive linkage in the feedback mechanism to rotate the gear drive to the characterising cam. Movement of this cam causes the spring beam mechanism to rotate about its pivot and readjusts the pilot valve assembly, moving it down towards its original position, eventually cutting off the air supply to the diaphragm so that the air pressure trapped above the diaphragm balances the force exerted by the main valve spring and the main valve attached to the valve spindle is held in its new position. This particular arrangement is direct acting (an increase in the control pressure signal causes the diaphragm pressure to increase). It can be made reverse acting by removing the plug in the lower port of the pilot valve and placing it in the top port. Clockwise movement of the pilot beam then opens the diaphragm to atmosphere, the diaphragm pressure drops and the valve spindle moves up. This is usually done by two small valves on the actuator rather than actually moving the plugs.

In some 'fast' control systems a positioner may not be used, and even if valve friction is high the use of a positioner can result in poorer performance of the system.

Whether a system is 'fast' or 'slow' a positioner will have to be used if it is necessary to adjust the pressure at which the valve starts to open or close

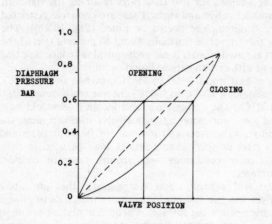

Fig. 101(a) Hysteresis Loop

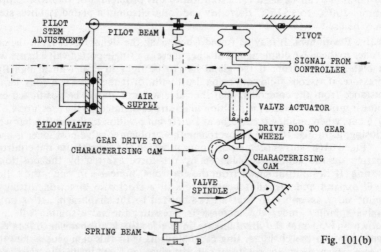

Fig. 101(b)

(adjustment A), or to control the range of diaphragm pressure to move the valve from open to close, or close to open, i.e. to provide the facility for split range control. A positioner would also be used to supply air at a higher pressure than the standard pressure in the system, for increased thrust.

For a non-linear cam the valve may move more or less depending upon the cam shape. By using cams of different shape, the rate of flow relative to the controller output pressure can be adjusted so that the performance of the valve can be adjusted to the system requirements. Such problems as instability due to an oversized valve or the characteristic of the valve not matching that of the controller or plant can be dealt with in this way. The cams are sometimes called characterization cams (Fig. 101(c)) and matching process 'characterizing'.

Remote indication of valve position is best taken direct from the valve stem. This can be by limit switches operated by the spindle at the extremes of the valve stroke or, if intermediate position indication is required, by a potentiometer or an inductance ratio device.

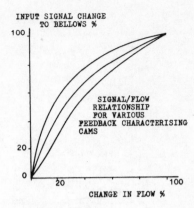

Fig. 101(c) Valve Characterising

Fig. 101(d) Force Balance Positioner

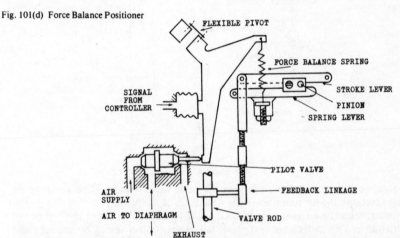

Fig. 101(d) shows a force balance type where, if an increasing pressure is applied to the input bellows, the bell crank lever rotates anti-clockwise and the pilot valve increases the air supply to the actuator. The resultant valve stem motion is transferred via the feedback linkage and the positioner levers to the force balance spring, loading it until the spring tension on the bell crank lever balances the opposing force on the bellows. When these two forces balance each other, the system is in equilibirum. When the stroke setting has been established, any given controller output pressure in the bellows forces the stem to take a corresponding position to maintain the pilot in the throttling position.

Piston Actuators are used for applications where high unbalanced forces make powerful actuators, possibly using high air pressures, desirable. Where a single ported valve is required because of tight shut-off requirements or improved flow characteristics, but high out-of-balance forces exist, such an actuator would be necessary. They provide a long stroke, fast powerful action, and can be used with high air pressures, up to 10·5 bar. Fig. 102 shows a basic layout of such an actuator. Under equilibrium conditions the pilot valve is in mid-position blocking off both ports. A decrease in controller output pressure for example,

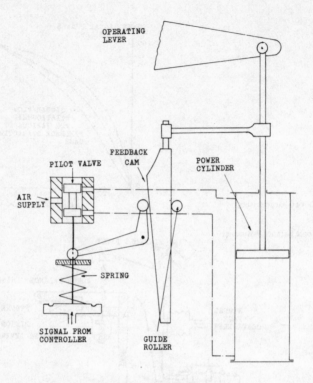

Fig. 102 Piston Actuator

moves the diaphragm down carrying the pilot valve with it. High pressure air flows through the bottom port to the underside of the piston, forcing this up the cylinder, with the air from the topside going to atmosphere over the top of the pilot valve. This movement is transmitted to the control spring by the cam and bell crank lever and continues until the force exerted by the spring balances the force exerted on the diaphragm. The pilot valve is then back in the mid or null position.

If the piston is affected by an opposing force, its movement will not be prevented as the pilot valve remains open until the air pressure is sufficient to overcome the force and the piston only stops when its position meets the requirements of the controller output pressure, as with the diaphragm actuator. Various shaped cams can be used to give a particular desired relationship between control pressure and piston position.

Butterfly valves are used in systems where a very small pressure drop across the valve is required, and in low head systems, as they give a very good recovery of the pressure drop between the inlet and vena contractor.

For control purposes, the flow characteristic is only suitable for control from about 10° to 60°, although with the 'Fishtail' design this can be extended up to 90°. This design also improves the resistance to cavitation damage. The characteristic is of the equal percentage form, and a high proportion of the flow is directed towards the trailing edge of the disc, giving an uneven pressure

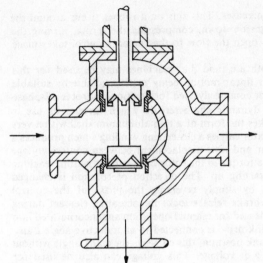

Fig. 103 Three way valve

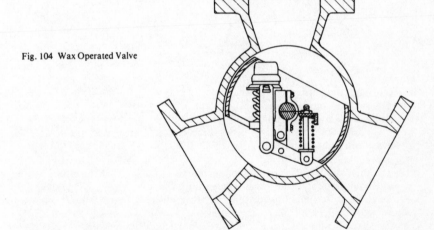

Fig. 104 Wax Operated Valve

distribution over the upstream and downstream sides. A torque is thus produced which tends to close the valve. Fig. 103 shows a three-way valve.

Fig. 104 shows a wax operated valve frequently used in temperature control applications, where the valve acts as means of controlling the flow of fluid passing through and by-passing a cooler.

The whole of the actuating mechanism is immersed in the fluid, temperature control being achieved by means of a copper capsule containing a wax which expands as the temperature increases, This acts on a rubber sleeve around the top of a piston, forcing the piston down, compressing the spring, turning the valve to shut the by-pass and open the flow to the cooler. Control takes place over about 10°C.

Electric Valve Actuators. Both a.c. and d.c. machines may be used for this purpose, with either rotary or linear motion being made available by suitable gearing arrangements. A motor commonly used for position control is a 2-phase a.c. machine with a special dynamic characteristic which favours its use in control systems. The rotor takes the form of a thin aluminium shell with a very low moment of inertia. The stator carries a closed ring winding which produces a rotating field through angular and time displacement between control voltage and excitation; this generates a torque in the rotor eddy current action, reaching its maximum value during starting up. The direction of rotation is changed without mechanical contacts by simply reversing the phase of the control voltage. An electro-magnetic brake release locks the actuating element during mains failure, and it can be released for manual operation and incorporated into any interlock system. The crank drive is connected to an inductive angle transmitter for feeding back the crank position; this converts the crank angle without contacts into a proportional a.c. voltage. This voltage can also be used for remote indication of the crank position.

CHAPTER 11

Control Systems—Steam and Motor

Boiler Water Level Control. Modern high pressure, high performance water tube boilers present a considerable number of problems with regard to the control of water level. The drums are relatively small in size and water capacity but have high outputs, whilst the reaction of the steam and water in the drum to changes in steam demand and hence drum pressure, are complex. A sudden increase in steam demand reduces the steam pressure in the drum, and to drop the temperature of the water to a saturation temperature matching the new pressure, some of the water flashes off into steam causing the formation of a mass of steam bubbles which tends to increase the drum level. The situation is aggravated by an increase in evaporation rate due to the increase in the temperature difference (and thus heat transfer rate) due to the drop in saturation temperature between the water in the tubes and the furnace and gas temperature. The effect is known as *swell* and on a simple level control system would cause the feed control valve to shut in—when in fact it should be opening—making it 180° out of phase.

When the boiler load levels out, and the combustion system restores the pressure, the saturation temperature also rises, the steam bubble formation (ebullition) drops and the level falls. Comparatively cold incoming feed water, as the feed valve opens, will cause some steam bubble collapse, and *shrinkage* of the level can occur. With the small drum of some boilers this can upset water circulation and cause heating surfaces to be uncovered.

To overcome the problem, *Two Element* feed water control has been devised (not to be confused with *two term* which applies to a proportional and reset controller). Here steam flow is measured by an orifice plate or flow nozzle and working on the basis that for a state of equilibrium feed flow into a boiler must equal steam flow out, the steam flow (the first element of the system) is used to position the feed water control valve. This valve is characterized so that for a given steam flow signal it is positioned to give a matching feed water flow. To allow for blowdown, leakage, perhaps soot blowing, etc., and for the time delay between a change in steam demand and the feed water control valve moving, a second element, a level sensor and transmitter is used. This sends a signal to a two-term controller which 'trims' the feed water control valve to restore the level should it deviate. Thus, for a change in steam demand, the flow transmitter produces a signal which is introduced into the control system by a summation relay and operates the feed water control valve. If the change in loading is large, the steam flow signal change will be equally large, and the effects of swell and shrinkage much less. Any subsequent change in level will be dealt with by the level controller via the summating relay. Fig. 105 shows the basic system.

Three Element Control. In the previous system it is necessary to maintain a constant feedwater pressure at the inlet of the regulating valve to optimize operation. Any fluctuation in feed water pressure will affect the drum level and this control will then try to adjust the regulating valve to restore the desired level condition. This could cause cyclic conditions in the system, over working

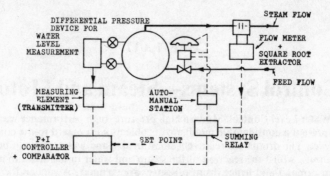

Fig. 105 Two Element Boiler Water Level Control

components and compounding the trouble. A third element is therefore introduced, namely feed water flow. Basing the operation upon the fact that for equilibrium steam flow must equal feed water flow both of these conditions are monitored and the signals compared in a differential relay, and provided they are equal, the output of this is then added to the desired value of the water level

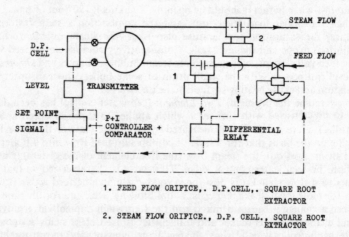

1. FEED FLOW ORIFICE,. D.P.CELL,. SQUARE ROOT
                                    EXTRACTOR

2. STEAM FLOW ORIFICE., D.P. CELL., SQUARE ROOT
                                    EXTRACTOR

Fig. 106 Three Element Boiler Water Level Control

in the drum. This signal is then compared with the drum level measured value signal in the two-term controller, and any deviation between the measured value and the desired value plus the difference between the steam and feed flows will cause the controller to reposition the feed water control valve to restore the level.

When there is an increase in steam demand, the differential relay is unbalanced and demands a higher drum level, counterbalancing the swell effect and trying to close the feed water control valve. When the steam flow falls, the differential relay is again unbalanced and demands a low level and alters the shrinkage effect. Any variation in feedwater flow due to pressure fluctuation will be detected by the flowmeter, repositioning the valve before the drum level is affected. With this system it is also possible to provide a variable level set point depending upon load—higher level as load increases and also high and low signal limits to optimize the setting of the system to account for boiler dynamics under arduous manoeuvring conditions. The basic loop is shown in Fig. 106 and may be used in conjunction with a system measuring the pressure drop across the feed water control valve and adjusting the turbo-feed pump steam valve to keep the feed water pressure contact.

It will be seen that square root extractors have been incorporated on both steam flow and feed flow signals to linearize them, as flow measurements by flow nozzle or orifice plate have a square root function of the pressure drop across these. Fig. 107 shows a mass/level control system in which the total mass of water is measured and the feed water control valve positioned to maintain this constant. A drum level trimming feature is also incorporated.

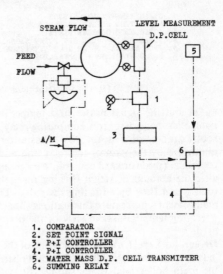

Fig. 107 Mass Level Control System

1. COMPARATOR
2. SET POINT SIGNAL
3. P+I CONTROLLER
4. P+I CONTROLLER
5. WATER MASS D.P. CELL TRANSMITTER
6. SUMMING RELAY

Superheater Steam Temperature control systems will depend on the type of boiler. In some designs dampers regulate the combustion gas flow through the superheat section of the uptake. A sensor on the superheat steam outlet pipe monitors the superheat steam temperature, sending its signal via a transmitter and comparator to a controller. The output signal from this goes to a computing relay which is also connected to receive a signal from a square-root extractor of a steam flow sensor/transmitter.

The relay exaggerates the temperature controller reaction when rapid load changes occur whilst the flow signal is only active during load changes and supplies a signal proportional to rate of change of steam flow. The output of the computing relay positions the damper actuator. Fig. 108 shows a system where a drum attemperator controls the superheat steam temperature. Here a fixed restriction (orifice plate) gives a resistance equivalent to that of a control valve in the fully open position. The superheat steam temperature is measured at the

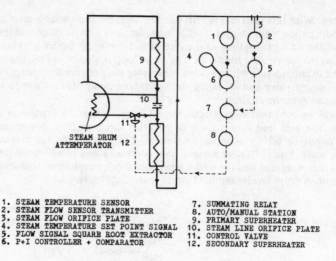

1. STEAM TEMPERATURE SENSOR
2. STEAM FLOW SENSOR TRANSMITTER
3. STEAM FLOW ORIFICE PLATE
4. STEAM TEMPERATURE SET POINT SIGNAL
5. FLOW SIGNAL SQUARE ROOT EXTRACTOR
6. P+I CONTROLLER + COMPARATOR
7. SUMMATING RELAY
8. AUTO/MANUAL STATION
9. PRIMARY SUPERHEATER
10. STEAM LINE ORIFICE PLATE
11. CONTROL VALVE
12. SECONDARY SUPERHEATER

Fig. 108 Superheat Steam Temperature Control

outlet and the signal passes to a temperature controller. The outlet from this controller then passes to a computing relay, to which the output from the square root extractor of a steam flow transmitter is also passed. This latter signal is multiplied by the gain of the relay and added to the output of the temperature controller (feed forward control). Any change in output pressure of the relay will alter the amount of steam flowing through the attemperator in relation to the total steam flow by adjusting the valve. This valve would fail safe open. Normally steam temperature fluctuations should not exeed±5°C, particularly at high operating temperatures in view of the permissable temperatures of the material used.

De-aerator Level Control. This is one of the most important level control systems in the steam plant. Any lack of stability here would cause serious disturbances in the main boiler feed water supply. Fig. 109 shows a control system for controlling de-aerator water level, this being measured by a differential pressure level sensor (dp cell) and transmitter, the signal being sent to a controller which operates two valves on split range control in such a way that a dead band of about 50 mm in level exists when both valves are closed. A rise in de-aerator water level opens the spill valve allowing water from the feed system to enter the distilled water tanks. A fall in level in the de-aerator causes the make-up valve to open, allowing water to flow from these tanks to the atmospheric drain tank. A stable level is maintained easily at high loads due to the rapid water flow in the feed system and changes easily detected, but at low loads, when water flow is sluggish, some time may elapse before the level alters sufficiently to open one of the valves. Should an air failure occur, the spill valve fails safe shut and the make-up valve fails-safe open.

Atmospheric Drain Tank. Control may be carried out by a combination of on-off switches and a level transmitter and controller. (Fig. 110)

At sea the flow through the drains tank is low and can be dealt with by the line to the condenser, controlled by the level controller passing a signal to a solenoid-

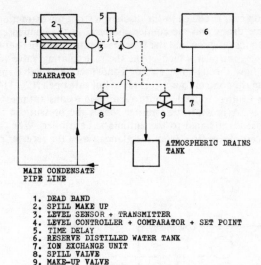

DEAERATOR

MAIN CONDENSATE
PIPE LINE

ATMOSPHERIC DRAINS
TANK

1. DEAD BAND
2. SPILL MAKE UP
3. LEVEL SENSOR + TRANSMITTER
4. LEVEL CONTROLLER + COMPARATOR + SET POINT
5. TIME DELAY
6. RESERVE DISTILLED WATER TANK
7. ION EXCHANGE UNIT
8. SPILL VALVE
9. MAKE-UP VALVE

Fig. 109 De-Aerator Level Control

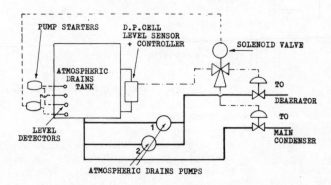

Fig. 110 Atmospheric Drain Tank Level Control

operated three-way control valve. This operates a valve on the line to the condenser to maintain the tank level at about 25 per cent full. If the capacity of this line is exceeded and the level rises, a float switch operates one pump and excess water is discharged to the de-aerator until the level drops and the level controller takes over.

When the flow through the tank is high, such as when deck steam or cargo pumps are being used, one drains pump would probably be running continuously on hand and the level is controlled by the level controller acting on the discharge valve to the condenser. When there is an excessive flow the float switch cuts in the second pump. Hunting of this pump is prevented by the level controller action regulating the pump output.

Air Ejector Recirculation Control is required to prevent the ejector condenser overheating and loss of vacuum. A flow sensing orifice and differential pressure transmitter (dp cell) is placed in the discharge from the extraction pumps. When the steam flow drops and the condensate level in the condenser well falls, the pumps tend to lose suction and the flow transmitter (at a pre-set flow rate) sends a signal to the controller which opens the recirculating valve to the condenser locating the flow through the ejector condenser. The valve may be remotely operated from the control room. It is set to fail safe open (Fig. 111(a)).

Gland Steam Control is carried out to maintain a constant pressure in the gland steam receiver. A pressure transmitter senses the pressure in the gland steam receiver and sends a signal to the automatic controller. When steaming under full load, excess steam flow from the glands raises the receiver pressure and the

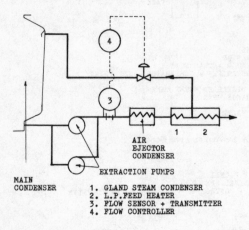

MAIN
CONDENSER

AIR
EJECTOR
CONDENSER

EXTRACTION PUMPS

1. GLAND STEAM CONDENSER
2. L.P.FEED HEATER
3. FLOW SENSOR + TRANSMITTER
4. FLOW CONTROLLER

Fig. 111(a) Air Ejector Re-Circulation Control

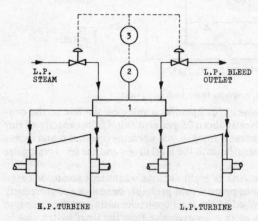

L.P.
STEAM

L.P. BLEED
OUTLET

H.P.TURBINE   L.P.TURBINE

1. GLAND STEAM RECEIVER
2. PRESSURE SENSOR + TRANSMITTER
3. P+I CONTROLLER + COMPARATOR + SET POINT

Fig. 111(b) Turbine Gland Steam Control

controller, at a pre-set pressure, opens the dump valve to the LP turbine bleed connnection. Under reduced load conditions the receiver pressure drops and steam is supplied from a reduced pressure steam line to the receiver and glands via a control valve, the opening of which is adjusted to give the required receiver pressure.

This valve and the dump valve act on split range control, with a dead band so that both valves are not open together. The dump valve is fail safe shut, the control valve fail safe open (Fig. 111(b)).

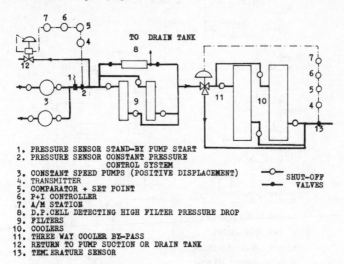

1. PRESSURE SENSOR STAND-BY PUMP START
2. PRESSURE SENSOR CONSTANT PRESSURE
   CONTROL SYSTEM
3. CONSTANT SPEED PUMPS (POSITIVE DISPLACEMENT)
4. TRANSMITTER
5. COMPARATOR + SET POINT
6. P+I CONTROLLER
7. A/M STATION
8. D.P.CELL DETECTING HIGH FILTER PRESSURE DROP
9. FILTERS
10. COOLERS
11. THREE WAY COOLER BY-PASS
12. RETURN TO PUMP SUCTION OR DRAIN TANK
13. TEMPERATURE SENSOR

─○─ SHUT-OFF
─●─ VALVES

PUMPS INCORPORATE SPRING LOADED BY-PASS VALVES

Fig. 111(c) Lubricating Oil Pressure and Temperature Control System

Fig. 111(c) shows a temperature control system and pressure control system for lubricating oil.

Automatic Combustion Control. In order to improve the response of high capacity boiler plant to fast changes in loadings whilst maintaining stability, the primary signal to the control loop may be taken from a steam flow sensor/transmitter. This would be in the form of a flow orifice or nozzle, possibly in the boiler saturated steam pipe, with the pressure drop being measured by a differential pressure transmitter in conjunction with a square root extractor to make the output signal (measured value of steam flow) linear, or proportional to steam flow and thus compatible with the other control system signals. This signal is then fed into the computing relay (Fig. 112a).

The steam pressure, either at the drum or superheater outlet, is measured by a steam pressure sensor/transmitter. The output signal from this (measured value of steam pressure) is fed to the master steam pressure controller, a two-term (P + I) controller. Here, this measured value signal is compared with the signal representing the desired value of steam pressure. Any deviation signal is fed into the computing relay. The master steam pressure controller acts as a trimming effect on the firing rate, prevents any prolonged deviation from the desired value steam pressure and overcomes any deficiency in the steam flow signal accuracy which can occur at low loads.

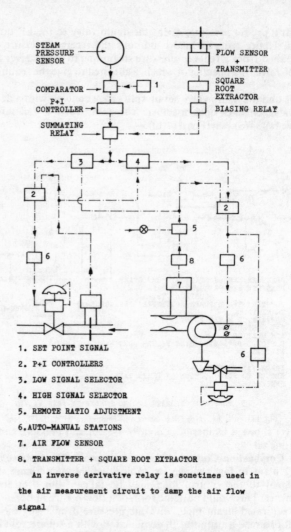

1. SET POINT SIGNAL

2. P+I CONTROLLERS

3. LOW SIGNAL SELECTOR

4. HIGH SIGNAL SELECTOR

5. REMOTE RATIO ADJUSTMENT

6. AUTO-MANUAL STATIONS

7. AIR FLOW SENSOR

8. TRANSMITTER + SQUARE ROOT EXTRACTOR

An inverse derivative relay is sometimes used in the air measurement circuit to damp the air flow signal

Fig. 112(a) Automatic Combustion Control System

The computing relay (adding or subtracting) output is now the steam flow signal plus, or minus, the steam pressure signal, depending upon whether the steam pressure is high or low. This master signal represents the fuel input requirements to the boiler. This is then fed as a variable desired value signal to each of the two-term controllers in the fuel control loop and the combustion air control loop, via a high/low signal selector system. This ensures that when a change of load occurs, the combustion air flow is always in excess of the fuel requirements to prevent bad combustion and smoke. The problem arises due to the fast response of the fuel oil loop to a load change, compared to the slow response of the combustion air loop.

The master signal passing to the fuel flow controller is fed through a low signal selector where it is compared with the signal representing the air flow. If this master signal is lower, the selector passes it and the two-term controller operates the fuel flow control valves. If the signal is higher, the low signal selector blocks it and there is no change in the signal to these valves.

In the passing to the FD fan two-term controller, via a high signal selector, the master signal is compared with a signal representing fuel flow, and if it is lower than the latter it is blocked, if higher, passed on. The controller then operates the louvre positioner and actuator and/or the fan speed positioner and actuator. Thus, for a rising steam load the increasing master signal to the fuel oil flow and combustion air controllers is fed firstly to the high/low signal selectors. At the high signal selector it is passed on to the FD fan controller which acts to increase the combustion air flow. This increase is detected by an air flow transmitter, the signal output from this being made proportional to air flow by a square root extractor. This signal then acts on the air flow controller, being compared to new desired value set by the master signal and adjusting the air flow until a balance is achieved.

The signal representing air flow is also passed to the low signal selector which, on detecting an increase in combustion air supply to the boiler, switches over to pass the master signal to the fuel oil controller. The master signal then adjusts the desired value of this and so increases the fuel flow. The increase is then measured by a flow orifice, a dp cell and the signal, via a square root extractor, passes to the fuel flow controller where it is compared with the new desired value signal, the output signal then being adjusted to achieve a balance.

Fuel to air ratio requirement is fed into the combustion air flow signal from the air flow transmitter. The fuel flow may be controlled by two valves in split range to give good control over a wide operating range. The combustion air flow may initially be controlled by vanes on the air inlet to the fans and then on fan speed.

Switches may be operated by the steam pressure signal to cut out the steam flow transmitter signal if the safety valve lifting pressure is approached.

For a decreasing steam load the master signal representing the fuel oil requirement is passed initially only to the oil fuel flow controller. Arrangements can be made to prevent the 'base' burner being lost at low oil fuel flow due to controller saturation by means of a cut off relay in the line from the controller to the valve. Fig. 112(b) shows basis of a burner light-up programme. Conditions which allow or prevent any automatic procedure from continuing are known as 'permissive interlocks', i.e. permission is given or refused depending upon whether or not a required condition is attained.

Bridge Control System. Such a system for a turbine plant invariably involves a closed loop rpm feedback system in which the desired propeller rpm is selected at the bridge control station and a proportional signal fed into a controller (usually two-term). Here it is compared with the measured value signal representing the actual propeller rpm. Any difference between the two signals produces an error signal which is then used to re-adjust the manoeuvring valve to supply the correct amount of steam to the turbine to give the required propeller rpm. Manoeuvring speed is carried out by adjusting the desired valve at the bridge station, the signal range being split to provide the ahead or astern direction required, i.e. (60 rpm astern, $0·35$ bar—zero rpm., $0·63$ bar—85 rpm. Ahead, $1·05$ bar). Electronic systems could be similarly split, using 0–10mA or 4–20mA ranges for example.

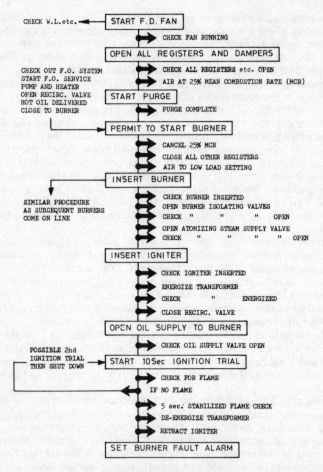

Fig. 112(b) Burner Light-up Programme

Automatic control of propeller rpm can also be carried out from the engine-room control station, as well as remote positioning of the maneouvring valves should the control circuit fail. Local hand operation facilities should also be provided at the manoeuvring valves.

Certain constraints have to be built into the control system to allow for problems involving both boiler and turbine operation. For the boiler, lifting of the safety valves should be avoided due to extremely fast speed reduction, whilst thermal inertia, shrink and swell of water level, and carry-over create limiting factors on the rate of manoeuvring valve movement.

With the turbine, excessive stress at the blade roots and gear tooth roots, scuffing of gear teeth under poor lubrication conditions and differential expansion and thermal inertia of casings and rotors, particularly when running astern for prolonged periods or when working up from full ahead to full away, have to be taken into account.

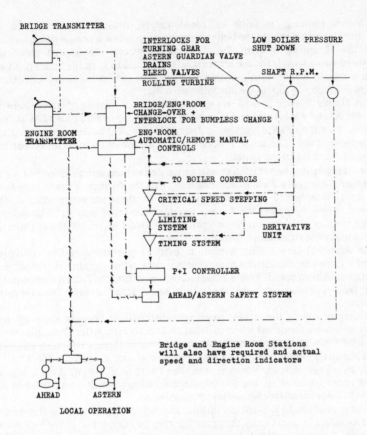

Fig. 113 Turbine Bridge Control System

Fig. 113 shows a basic system in which the bridge transmitter when on bridge control, transmits the desired value signal to give the required propeller rpm. The engine room transmitter is in the 'bridge control' position and the respective indicators show this illuminated. The engine room may override the bridge at any time, this is carried out by switching the bridge control system to engine room control and placing the latter transmitter at the required rpm indicated by the bridge order follower. The respective 'engine room in control' indicators are now illuminated and manoeuvring orders would be transmitted by the bridge to the engine room via an indicating system, such as a telegraph, with audible alarms.

The control station in the engine control room provides the means for remote manual control, with bumpless change-over. The desired value signal is then fed into the control system where, according to the change in rpm required and hence the strength of the signal, the various restraints are brought into operation, as well as the interlocks indicated. These may include: preventing the turbine operating in the critical speed range, making sure the turning gear is disengaged (essential interlock) and ensuring the astern guardian valve is open

113

for astern running, position of bleed valves, drains and closing in the manoeuvring valve should the boiler pressure drop below a pre-set value.

In the **'Limiting System'** the difference between the desired value and measured value signals (or the error signal) is limited to keep the boiler pressure, water level and turbine torque within safe limits by preventing the rate of change of power becoming too high whilst manoeuvring.

The **Timing System** is used to regulate the rate of change of power between *Full Ahead* and *Full Away* and vice-versa. It only comes into operation at shaft speeds higher than *Full Ahead* being designed to prevent boiler over-loading and safety valve lifting. The action is achieved by a system of resistors and capacitors giving a time delay to the signal.

For emergencies the bridge transmitter may be moved into an *Emergency Full Astern* or *Emergency Full Ahead* position. For the former, a crash stop from Full Away is achieved by a switch operated by the transmitter when in this position, which by-passes the Timing System. The latter may be achieved in a similar manner or by means of an audible and visual alarm for the engineering staff to make the required adjustment.

The Ahead/Astern Safety System is used to prevent excessive cavitation caused by opening the Astern manoeuvring valve when the ship is travelling at too high an Ahead speed. This is achieved by preventing the Astern manoeuvring valve from opening until the shaft rpm has reached a safe limit (approx. 30 rpm).

Blasting or rolling the turbine to prevent distortion is brought about by time delays which are energized when the shaft comes to rest. After three minutes at rest these time delays produce 'false' desired value signals which in sequence rotate the shaft alternately up to 5 rpm ahead or astern. Sometimes the 'blast' is timed, 10–15 secs Ahead, 3 minute stop then 10–15 secs Astern. If the bridge or engine room transmitters are moved the time delays are de-energized and the system becomes available for normal manoeuvring.

In some systems, to prevent the turbine and boiler control systems fluctuating as the motion the ship causes the propeller rpm to vary, when in the Full Away condition the rpm feedback is switched out and manoeuvring valve position control is employed.

A closed loop test circuit is incorporated to enable a complete system test to be carried out without interrupting the operating of the control system. In modern systems the combustion control, water level control, steam pressure and temperature and manoeuvring control systems are interlinked to provide an integrated control system matched to the propeller, turbine and boiler characteristics.

DIESEL ENGINE SYSTEMS

Fig. 114 shows the basic requirements for starting and control of a direct reversing slow speed diesel engine. The basic control loop for diesel engine is of closed loop form with a two- or three-term controller, possibly with a load limiting device and alarm, controlling the engine speed. Desired value signals for engine rpm are transmitted from the bridge control position or engine room remote control position and compared with the measured value signal from a propeller shaft speed sensor, the difference between these two signals being the rpm deviation from that required. This error signal is then used by the controller

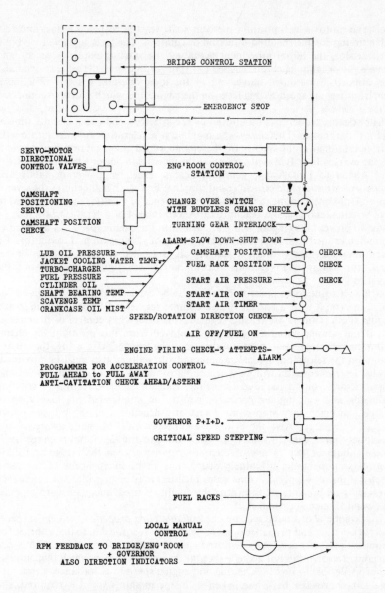

Fig. 114 Direct Reversing Diesel Engine Bridge Control System

to adjust the fuel racks to return the engine speed to that required. Electronic electro-pneumatic, electro hydraulic and pneumatic systems may be used for signal transmission and fuel rack operation.

In Fig. 114 the direction of rotation required is achieved by moving a lever in a horizontal slot, movement to either extreme operating the valves controlling the servo-motor which position the cam shaft for the correct air start and fuel valve timing for the required direction of rotation. The lever is then moved in a vertical slot, the initial movement actuating the starting sequence on air and when a pre-set rpm has been reached (30 rpm for example) the air is tripped and fuel applied. Subsequent movement of the lever operates a servo-mechanism which adjusts the speed setting lever on the engine and which is in turn connected to the governor.

The starting sequence is monitored by the interlock and check circuits shown, and a programmer. This allows the maximum acceleration commensurate with safe operational requirements of the engine whilst manoeuvring but prevents engine overloading. It also programmes the increase in power when moving from Full Ahead to Full Away, guarding against excessive power demands and propeller cavitation and critical speed slipping. For crash manoeuvres the lever is moved from one extreme to the other, the sequence of events is then controlled to give braking, starting and reaching full speed (ahead or astern). Delays may be fitted to prevent braking air being applied until the engine speed has dropped to a pre-determined rpm to prevent excessive use of starting air and cavitation. An alarm may be fitted to warn if starting air is applied to the engine for longer than, for example, 15 seconds. Crash manoeuvre signals may cut-out the governor.

Bridge/Engine room control transfer may be carried out by the bridge-engine room telegraph with a special bridge control segment. When both bridge and engine room pointers are on this segment, the bridge has control of the engine, but if the pointer on either telegraph is moved from this position, the engine room has control, and manoeuvring may be carried out using the engine room/bridge telegraph. Local manual control facilities also must be provided. Bridge instrumentation will vary according to the desires of the shipowner and manufacturer, but is required to include rpm indicator, direction of rotation indicator and starting air pressure, whilst for unattended machinery space vessels, an emergency stop control system independent of the bridge control system is required. Also the bridge watchkeeper must be made aware of any machinery fault, that the fault is being attended to and that it has been rectified. There should be two means of communication between the bridge and main control station in the machinery space, one to be independent of the main electrical power supply. In some cases facilities may be provided for emergency overriding oil pressure shutdown. If this facility is used, adequate warning must be given to the engine room staff.

In the control of vessels using a *controllable pitch propeller* the engine speed, fuel rack setting and propeller pitch are pre-set in relationship to one another for optimum performance. Any required change in ship speed or direction is obtained by the operation of a single lever at the control station which then adjusts the propeller pitch, fuel rack setting and engine speed in accordance with a pre-determined programme. Thus, when a change in ship's speed is required, the signal proportional to the change is fed to the governor and to the pitch setting mechanism. The fuel racks are adjusted and assuming the engine load does not exceed the pre-determined maximum for the speed chosen, the signal will adjust the pitch setting mechanism until the signal representing the actual pitch matches that of the desired pitch. Should there be an increase in load the engine speed will tend to drop, causing the governor to move the fuel racks so that the engine speed is restored. In moving the fuel racks the governor also moves a transducer which produces a signal proportional to the overload. This signal is then fed into the pitch control system via a relay which gives a bias to the desired pitch signal, so that it no longer matches the actual pitch signal and the error then operates the pitch setting servomotor and mechanism, adjusting the propeller pitch. This adjustment continues until the actual pitch and the new modified desired value pitch signals match and the engine operates around the new loading condition.

In the arrangement mechanism shown in Fig. 115, the input signal to the pitch change operates a variable stroke oil pump which pumps oil to the left-hand side of the piston and receives oil from the right-hand side, or vice-versa. As the

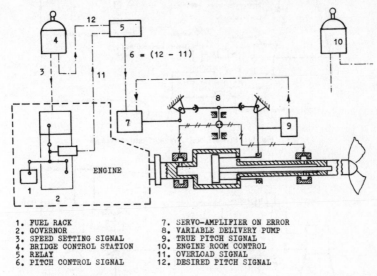

1. FUEL RACK
2. GOVERNOR
3. SPEED SETTING SIGNAL
4. BRIDGE CONTROL STATION
5. RELAY
6. PITCH CONTROL SIGNAL

7. SERVO-AMPLIFIER ON ERROR
8. VARIABLE DELIVERY PUMP
9. TRUE PITCH SIGNAL
10. ENGINE ROOM CONTROL
11. OVERLOAD SIGNAL
12. DESIRED PITCH SIGNAL

Fig. 115 Controllable Pitch Propeller Control System

piston moves it operates a feed-back mechanism which brings the pump stroke back to mid position, holding the piston and the propeller pitch at the required position. With UMS notation a propeller pitch and shaft rpm indicator should be fitted at each control station and means should be provided to prevent the engine and shafting being subjected to excessive torque due to changes in pitch. Alternatively an engine overload indicator should be similarly fitted. There should be an alternative power source for controlling the blade pitch. Audible and visual alarms should operate for: low hydraulic system pressure, low level in hydraulic supply tank, failure of power supply between bridge and hydraulic actuator and high oil temperature at the cooler outlet.

Piston Cooling Water inlet temperature control is shown in Fig. 116 where two temperature controllers are used in cascade with the output from the slave actuating two control valves in a split range arrangement. Should there be a failure of control air, the three-way control valve should be open to the cooler.

Fuel Valve Cooling Water inlet temperature control is shown in Fig. 117. Designed to keep the cooling water at constant temperature whilst the engine is running and for heating prior to starting, the controller is installed at the water inlet to the fuel valves, operating two control valves in split range. When running the steam valve is normally closed.

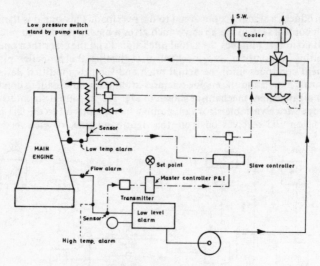

Fig. 116 Piston Cooling Water Control System

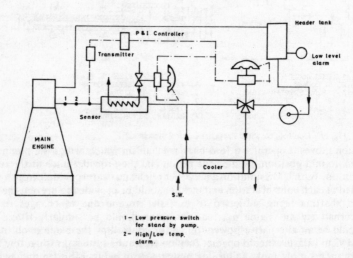

Fig. 117 Fuel Valve Cooling Water Control System

Lubricating Oil Temperature Control. The arrangement for this is shown in Fig. 118. The lubricating oil is pumped from the drain tank, very often with a magnetic filter in the suction line, via main suction filters, fitted with a differential pressure alarm. These filters may both be automatically cleaned or one hand-cleaned and one automatically.

In some cases, when the differential pressure exceeds a pre-set value, the filter is automatically back flushed with air, the displaced oil going to an auxiliary drains tank where it is subsequently filtered and pumped back into the system. Cooling is carried out by a three-way by-pass valve in the oil line controlled from

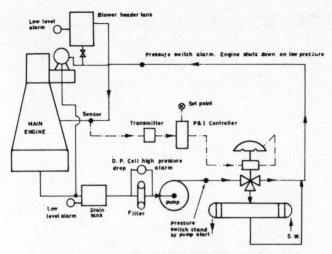

Fig. 118 Lubricating Oil Temperature Control System

a sensor at the inlet to the engine. This valve should fail safe with all the oil going through the cooler. In some arrangements the filters are placed after the coolers. Temperature monitoring would be carried out on the common inlet temperature, thrust inlet temperature, and blower outlet temperatures, all having alarms for high temperature. Low pressure is monitored at the common inlet to the engine with alarm and slowdown or shut down of the main engine. In some cases there may be an alarm only for low pressure on all supplies other than to the main bearings, with alarm and shut down only on these.

Low level is monitored on the drains tank and header tank by magnetic switches with a 20 second delay to prevent false alarms due to surging. Failure of the circulating pumps is alarmed, as is high differential pressure across the filters. Crankcase oil most detection alarm on high density with engine shut down. The lubricating oil purifier may take oil from the drains tank and discharge the clean oil into the supply line. The purifier is provided with a level alarm. If the water seal falls below a pre-set level an audible alarm is given and the purifier stopped. In some cases, if the sea water pressure falls, this also operates an alarm.

The *Butterworth Tank cleaning sea water heaters* present a problem with regard to maintaining a constant temperature due to the large quantities of sea water flowing at high velocity. The system shown in Fig. 119 has been developed such that the temperature of the sea water at the outlet from the heaters is monitored and supplies a signal to a master controller with proportional plus reset settings. The output from this provides the set point signal for a controller (the slave) in the heating steam supply line. Any variation in outlet SW temperature causes the master controller to adjust the set point of the slave controller, which in turn adjusts the steam supply to the heaters. Should there be a fluctuation in steam supply pressure, the slave controller senses this and readjusts the valve to restore the correct pressure at the heater. The level of condensate in the heaters is also monitored and kept constant by a controller adjusting a control valve. Sea water flow may be monitored, the heaters shut down

119

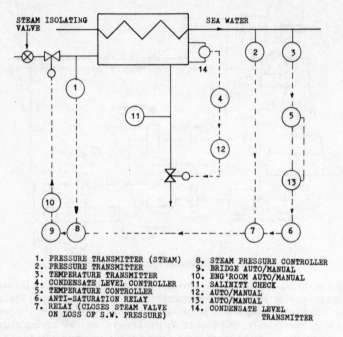

STEAM ISOLATING VALVE

SEA WATER

1. PRESSURE TRANSMITTER (STEAM)
2. PRESSURE TRANSMITTER
3. TEMPERATURE TRANSMITTER
4. CONDENSATE LEVEL CONTROLLER
5. TEMPERATURE CONTROLLER
6. ANTI-SATURATION RELAY
7. RELAY (CLOSES STEAM VALVE
   ON LOSS OF S.W. PRESSURE)

8. STEAM PRESSURE CONTROLLER
9. BRIDGE AUTO/MANUAL
10. ENG'ROOM AUTO/MANUAL
11. SALINITY CHECK
12. AUTO/MANUAL
13. AUTO/MANUAL
14. CONDENSATE LEVEL
    TRANSMITTER

Fig. 119 Butterworth S.W. Heating Control System

if it falls below a pre-determined level.

Automatic Control of Alternators. This is shown in schematic form in Fig. 120. The load measuring circuits of each alternator are supplied with current and voltage signals which are then modified by the amplifier into a form suitable for use in the load error circuits where each individual alternator load is compared with the average load signal. If the alternator loadings are incorrect the engine governor settings are adjusted and the alternator speed adjusted to bring them into line. The trigger circuits are used to provide positive control action so that it does not shift between on and off modes.

Each alternator also feeds a signal representing the output of its load measuring circuit into a circuit which computes the mean load regardless of the number of alternators on load. This is used, as above, to detect any discrepancies in the load sharing by each machine, and also to initiate start-up sequences for the 2nd, 3rd and 4th duty machines as the load demand increases. The start sequence is often initiated at 75 per cent of full load for those sets connected whilst shut down of one alternator would leave three alternators on 66 per cent of full load, two alternators on 60 per cent and one alternator on 50 per cent. This difference in starting and stopping load values is incorporated so that the loadings on each set do not produce a starting procedure immediately after one machine has shut down.

Each circuit breaker opens at 10 per cent Full Load during shut down procedure, the individual alternator load signals initiated at 105 per cent maximum rated load, and automatically takes into account the number of

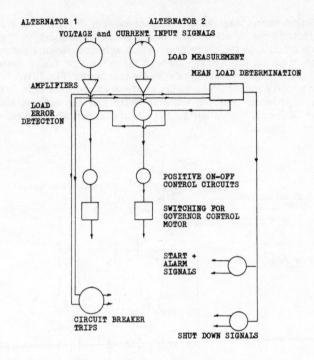

Fig. 120 Automatic Control of Alternators

machines on load. An overriding provision should be incorporated to ensure at least two alternators are sharing the load when in busy shipping lanes or narrow waters, thus giving a load safety margin. Also a short time delay of about 20 seconds may be incorporated to prevent starting on a false load demand.

Pre-start preparations must include lubricating oil priming, either by electrically or pneumatically driven pumps, whilst cylinder warming through is usually continuous from the main engine system. If a machine fails to pick up the load after two attempts, it is locked out and the next duty machine started and alarm is given of the failure of the first machine. Thus a machine is not repeatedly switched on to a short circuit, being locked out after connecting once.

Protection and alarms must be provided against maloperation of the engine and electrical faults and overloads, whilst preferential tripping of non-essential loads and subsequent restoration must be provided. Where minor faults do not warrant a shut down, alarm may be given before a shut down in a two-level circuit. Should a machine fail to start or shut down due to a malfunction, it should be locked out and alarm given.

Exhaust Gas Boiler Steam Pressure Control. Under normal steaming conditions the exhaust gas boiler supplies boiler feed, circulation, bilge and ballast pumps, heating and a turbo alternator at about 11 bars. Reducing valve (1) is fully open.

121

The circulation pump takes water from the bottom drum of the boiler and pumps it through the middle section of the exhaust gas boiler, returning the water steam mixture to the boiler drum which acts as a steam separator. The outlet steam from the drum passes through the exhaust gas boiler superheater, whilst incoming feed passes through this boiler economiser (Fig. 121).

When in port the main boiler supplies all steam at approximately 30 bars via its uptake superheater and the reducing valve and the exhaust gas boiler superheater. Valve (2) is normally shut at all times except when the exhaust gas boiler has to be isolated.

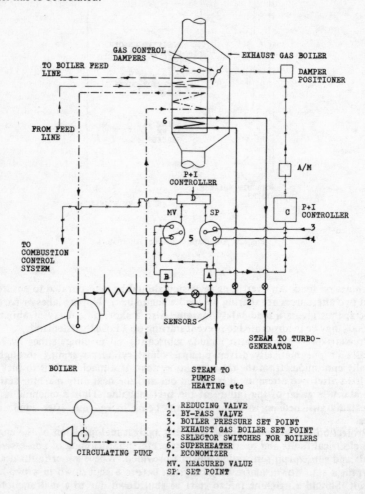

Fig. 121 Exhaust Gas Boiler Control System

1. REDUCING VALVE
2. BY-PASS VALVE
3. BOILER PRESSURE SET POINT
4. EXHAUST GAS BOILER SET POINT
5. SELECTOR SWITCHES FOR BOILERS
6. SUPERHEATER
7. ECONOMIZER
MV. MEASURED VALUE
SP. SET POINT

Steam pressure control when at sea is carried out through pressure transmitter (A) supplying a measured value signal through the selector switch (MV) to controller (D). If the measured value drops below the set point signal fed into

(D) this controller sends a signal to light up one burner in the boiler, which is on stand-by. Transmitter (A) also supplies a measured value signal to controller (C) which provides a signal to adjust the gas control dampers in the exhaust gas boiler to maintain the steam pressure.

In port when the boiler is in operation, the pressure transmitters (A) and (B) monitor the steam pressure. According to the set point entered into the system by the selector switch, the pressure of the main boiler will be maintained by controller (D) comparing the measured value steam pressure with the signal representing the set point steam pressure. This will control the FD fans, fuel oil pressure, and burner sequencing events.

Load Sensing Governor. When utilizing the speed of an alternator to control the fuel supply a problem arises with either proportional or proportional + reset modes of control in that there is no change in the control signal and hence the fuel supply until the speed actually changes. The addition of derivative control improves the governor performance as rate of change of speed then controls the fuel, but for the best results load changes should be used to control the fuel supply directly. This can easily be carried out with an electrical load, by measuring the load directly, monitoring the output of all three phases and then combining the total power to provide a signal to control the fuel supply. The signal thus produced is not part of the closed loop as the control of the prime mover speed is the main criterion and therefore speed sensing is still required to provide a means for maintaining the exact speed. The only time delays involved are those associated with the sensing elements and amplifier, either electric or hydraulic, needed to operate the fuel rack. By using load sensing governing, a considerable improvement in accuracy of control can be obtained. The

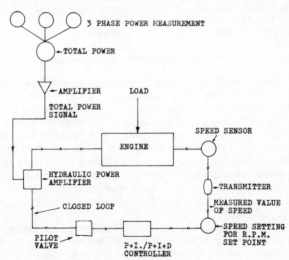

Fig. 122 Load Sensing Governor

arrangement uses a fast acting servo-mechanism to position the fuel rack or throttle proportionately to the load change. Should the load sensing fail a fast acting speed governor has also to be incorporated (Fig. 122).

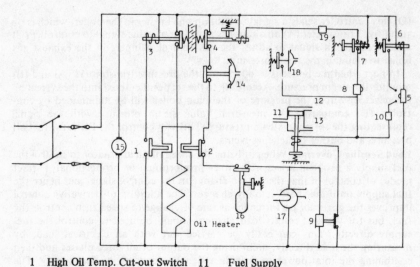

1	High Oil Temp. Cut-out Switch	11	Fuel Supply
2	Low Oil Temp. Cut-out Switch	12	Fuel to Burner
3	Oil Heater Switch	13	Fuel to Recirculating Line
	Flame Failure Cut-out Switch	14	Steam Pressure Switch
4	(hand reset)	15	Oil Pump
5	Photo Cell (Ignition Spark)		Low Water Level Cut-out
6	Ignition Circuit Switch	16	(hand reset)
7	Flame Failure Circuit Switch	17	F.D. Fan
8	Flame Failure Photo-cell		Combustion Air Failure Cut-out
9	Time Delay (Air Purge)	18	Switch
10	Timer (Ignition Spark)	19	Time Delay

Fig. 123 Auxiliary Boiler Control System

Fig. 123 shows a combustion control system for an auxiliary boiler operating on a simple ON-OFF cycle using a burner with a fixed throughput. When the main switch is closed, the oil pump starts, switch (3) remains closed under the influence of its spring thus completing the electrical oil heater circuit.

The oil distribution valve, under the influence of the spring is in the uppermost position so that oil circulates around the burner circuit and through the heater. A spring holds the flame failure cut out switch (4) closed, and when the oil reaches a pre-determined temperature, the low temperature thermostatic cut out switch (2) closes. When flashing up or when the steam pressure drops, switch (14) closes, and assuming the water level is correct, the fan circuit is made, starting the forced draught fan (17).

Time delay (9) prevents the oil fuel valve from being energized and moving to the lower position to supply oil to the burner until the furnace has been purged for three minutes. After the purge period, time delay (9) closes the solenoid which then moves the oil valve to the lower position, supplying oil to the burners. At the same time, the igniter is energized creating a spark, the circuit being closed by switch (6) under the influence of the spring. Time delay (10) limits the time the spark is present and if there is no flame at the burner in this period, the spark is de-energized and the flash up procedure re-starts. This may occur three times and then the system shuts down and an alarm is given. If the oil ignites, photocell (5) senses the flame at the burner tip, energizes the coil on switch (6) and opens this. At the same time, the establishment of the flame energizes photocell (8) which then passes a current to the coil on switch (7) opening this. Should the flame fail this photo-cell de-energizes the coil and the spring closes the switch which then energizes the circuit to switch (4) and opens this. This action de-energizes the coil on the fuel valve, shutting off the oil to the burners. Time delay (19) prevents immediate action to allow the igniter time to establish a flame. Should there be a combustion, air failure switch (18) will close, with a similar effect on switch (4).

CHAPTER 12

Monitoring Systems

Monitoring Systems vary considerably in size and complexity, simple circuits consisting of individual alarm lights operated by electrical contacts being opened or closed by a sensor, and usually activating an audible alarm. At the other end of the scale are the sophisticated types of equipment for alarm scanning (sequential monitoring of sensors and comparison with stored limit settings), data acquisition (collection of information on magnetic tape or punched paper tape stores for future reference and statistical analysis), data logging (printing out and displaying information on the conditions of the processes being monitored), and computing and control. These last two features would involve assessment of the operating conditions and automatic adjustment of the various processes to provide the optimum operating conditions for the prevailing conditions and requirements.

On the simple systems there are numerous modifications that may be fitted and these include locking in a fleeting alarm so that even though the alarm condition may have disappeared, it continues to be displayed. Automatic Reset or Manual Reset may be chosen (the latter requires manual resetting of the alarm once normal conditions have been restored) and 'First Up' or 'First Out' facilities can be provided, enabling the first alarm operated in a group to be identified when a number of alarms are displayed at any one time. Alarm presentation may be with normal operation—light out—siren off, fault—flashing light—siren on, accept alarm—steady light—siren off. Lamp test—steady light. Some designs use a dim light for normal operation, bright flashing for fault, bright steady light for accept and for 'first out' recognition a fast intermittent flashing light may be used, with a steady fast flash for subsequent faults, a slow flash for acceptance of the initial fault and steady for acceptance of subsequent faults. The siren sounds at initiation of all alarms.

The systems should be self-monitoring with a visual and audible alarm actuated if a conductor breaks in a two-wire system or sensor failure in a three-wire circuit. An events recorder which determines the order of occurrence of a sequence of alarms may also be fitted. The print-out records time of alarm, alarm channel and shows when normal operation is restored.

Fig. 124 shows a basic circuit for a monitoring system in which the signal from every analogue sensor passes into the measuring channel where it is amplified and adapted for digital and analogue readout. This channel is equipped with a comparator with adjustable voltages corresponding to the upper and lower limit values of the sensor signal. When either of these limits is exceeded the comparator emits a signal activating an audible and visual alarm. The analogue or measuring channel is built up from two circuit cards, one passive, the other active with a number of separate channels per card, each channel having its own sensor. The passive card contains resistors and capacitors only, the sensors being adapted by these which, for the temprature sensor, takes the form of a bridge

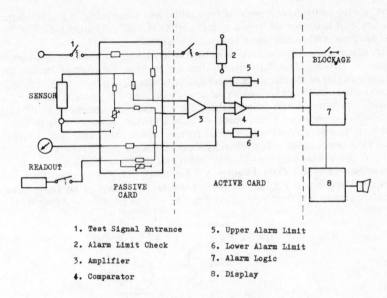

1. Test Signal Entrance
2. Alarm Limit Check
3. Amplifier
4. Comparator

5. Upper Alarm Limit
6. Lower Alarm Limit
7. Alarm Logic
8. Display

Fig. 124 Alarm Monitoring Circuit

connection, and for the pressure sensor, the form of a load resistance. Various further resistors determine amplification, connect outside instruments and serve as a voltage divider for the readout. It also includes circuits for operation check, alarm limit check and blockage.

The active card contains amplifiers and comparators as well as potentiometers for adjustment of the alarm limits. These potentiometers can be optionally set between the maximum and minimum measuring values. Whenever an alarm limit is passed the comparator transmits an alarm signal of approximately 3·5 V to the alarm circuit. The alarm circuit can be inhibited by connecting + 24 V to the blockage entrance. The amplifying parts of the circuit card are still operating when blocked, so that the measuring values can be read by pressing the button for the required channel and obtaining a reading on the digital voltmeter readout unit.

When carrying out an operation check, a blocking signal is momentarily impressed on a circuit card to eliminate a possible alarm on this particular channel, + 24 V are then connected to the operation check entrance whereby the amplifier is modulated to maximum and the comparator produces an alarm signal. One of the displays is furnished with a button for operation check.

During an alarm limit check a suitable voltage is impressed on the entrance of the amplifier via the potentiometer for alarm limit check on the active card. Pressing any of the test buttons on the card immediately connects the potentiometer, blocks the siren to avoid audible alarms and connects the channel to the reading unit for reading the alarm limit value.

When an alarm is released on a channel the associated lamp begins to flash and siren sounds. When stopping the alarm the alarm lamp glows continuously if the alarm persists and switches off if the alarm disappears. For analogue alarm channels the lamps have a push button facility and when pressure is applied the reading unit is connected within digital voltmeter and associated indicator for decimal point and measurement type to the channel.

To accept an alarm the siren stop button is pushed, followed by the accept alarm or flashing light button and then by pushing the channel button the measured value of the effending sensor can be obtained.

Suggested checks are as follows: *daily*—check lamps by pushing lamp check button, operation check, voltage check for the analogue channels (± ·02 volt acceptable) *monthly*—12 volt check on power circuit; *annually*—alarm limits check, analogue channels check with current sensor; this simulates a signal within the sensor range. Alarm channel check. Blockage channel check.

These checks may vary according to maker and shipowner's policy.

Alarm Scanners and **Data Loggers** are far more complex systems than the previous circuits and Fig. 125 shows a basic layout circuit of an alarm scanner/data acquisition, data logging system. The various conditions of the plant to

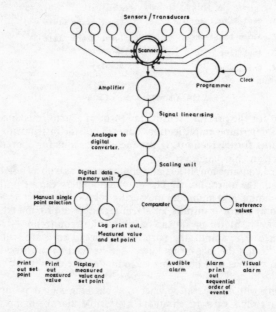

Fig. 125 Data Logger Layout

be monitored are sensed by suitable devices such as resistance thermometers, thermocouples, thermistors, strain gauges, differential transformers with Bourdon tubes, capacitance effect, dp cells, etc., producing an electrical signal current or voltage which is proportional to the measured value of the condition being monitored. These analogue inputs are fed into a scanner where each connection or point is automatically selected in a pre-determined sequence and the value of the signal passed on to the measuring circuits. The signal then passes to an amplifier where, whatever the form of the input in electrical terms, all the signals are within a common d.c. range at the output. The signal is still in analogue form (similar to the reading on a pressure gauge, the distance the pointer is away from zero on the gauge is the analogue of the pressure) and now has to be converted into digital form (similar to the milometer for a car where the distance travelled increases in pulses or steps). At the analogue to digital converter, the value of the signal is converted and represented by a series of electrical pulses.

Depending upon the scope of the equipment the signal may be diverted into two paths, one for alarm comparison, the other for data logging. In the alarm comparison circuit the signal is compared with pre-determined stored values set up in a comparator. Any shift in value then operates audible and visual alarms as with the previously described equipment and provides an alarm print out.

In the data logging channel the signal is prepared for print-out by being scaled so that it is presented in the correct units (i.e. bars, kN/m^2, °C), the required scaling factor being selected in the scaling unit for this purpose. The presentation may then be in typewritten form, or punched paper tape or on magnetic tape. Information can be obtained on visual instrumentation at any time as the scanner moves round the points or by pressing a button a typewritten presentation can be obtained. The machine can be set up to produce a complete log, for example every hour or every four hours or on demand. If a particular point required examination, by selecting it manually and pressing a button, the point will be repeatedly examined and its value presented. The rate of scanning is usually about 1 point per second although it can be reduced to 1 point every 3 seconds. There are various modifications offered by the manufacturers to suit particular applications.

Most units operate a self-check system where periodically a test signal is inserted and the circuits checked. The test circuit may also check itself. The advantages claimed for data-logging and alarm monitoring are: early warning of breakdown; close supervision gives improved efficiency; staff released from routine logging and recording duties; records of machinery behaviour under varying operating conditions; the acquisition of data providing information capable of analysis for future maintenance and design procedures.

Condition Monitoring. This is a development that the data logger has helped to produce, due to the vast amount of operational information compiled over a period of time by operators and manufacturers. The system incorporates a number of sensors on the engine and its auxiliaries, a system based on a micro-computer for data processing and a console where the computer results are displayed showing trends in plant performance, alarms or particular information required by the operator. The computer is pre-programmed with information on machinery behaviour analysed over a number of years of operation both from a manufacturer's observations and those of the operator. A continuous check is carried out on conditions such as air and gas flow, turbochargers and air coolers, combustion conditions, fuel injection, fuel consumption, engine output cylinder load distribution and vessels speed. Conditions such as wear and piston ring behaviour are also monitored as well as thermal load. Water and oil coolers in the auxiliary system are also monitored.

By carrying out a continuous check any abnormal operating conditions can be detected quickly and instructions issued to avoid further trouble and implement remedial action. It is anticipated that maintenance work would be organized on the basis of past experience and the actual trend in the condition of the particular components, thus avoiding unnecessary dismantling of machinery as frequently happens with maintenance work organized on a fixed time basis. For main engines should a monitored condition deviate from the normal condition, the monitor output is set in motion according to a pre-set programme.

CHAPTER 13

Semi-Conductor Devices

A semi-conductor is a material which is neither a conductor, nor an insulator and may loosely be described as having a resistivity 10^6 times that of a good conductor and 10^{-6} times that of a good insulator. When an electronic component operates due to the movement of electrons within a piece of solid semi-conductor material, then it is called a solid-state device.

The electrical properties of such semi-conductor materials depend upon the structure of their crystals and their electron bonding characteristics. It has been found that germanium and silicon have the most suitable crystal structure and bonding characteristics to make them useful for solid state electronic components adaptation. Pure germanium and silicon are of little use, but by adding or doping them with carefully controlled quantities of certain materials, their electrical characteristics can be altered and they then become very useful for a wide range of operations. Silicon has an advantage over germanium in that it can withstand higher temperatures and has a lower leakage current.

When a minute quantity of arsenic, antimony or phosphorous is added (or donated) to a piece of germanium or silicon, the crystal structure is adjusted so that the material has an abundance of electrons or free negative charges. This is called an N-type crystal. If a minute quantity of boron, aluminium or indium is added to the germanium or silicon, the crystal structure develops a defficiency of electrons and 'holes' are then said to have been made in the structure and these are considered to be mobile positive charges. This is then called a P-type crystal.

In an uncharged N semi-conductor there is an equal number of protons (+ charges) and electron (–charges) but some of the electrons available are not used for promoting bonds between the atoms and thus act as current carriers. In a similarly uncharged P material, again there is an equal number of protons and electrons, but this time there are not enough electrons to complete the bonding between nearby atoms and this allows 'holes' to develop, acting as carriers for an electric current.

If a piece of N-type material is placed touching a piece of P-type material, some of the surplus electrons from the N-type material will pass across the joint and combine with the holes of the P-type. Remembering that when separated they were both uncharged, this movement of electrons will continue until the difference in charges increases and the potential difference (or difference in the number of charges) reaches a point when further transfer is prevented. The area near the joint now becomes deficient in carriers of both types and it is called the barrier depletion layer or region (See Fig. 126).

If a potential difference is applied across the junction by connecting the P material to the negative terminal of the supply and N material to the positive terminal, thé holes will be attracted to the negative terminal and the electrons to the positive terminals and the P-type material is made more negative and the N-type material more positive. This action makes the depletion barrier wider and no current flows, except for a slight leakage current, and the junction is then said to be *reversed biased*, (see Fig. 127(a)).

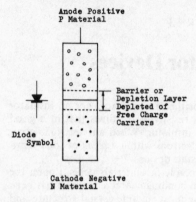

Anode Positive
P Material

Barrier or
Depletion Layer
Depleted of
Free Charge
Carriers

Fig. 126 P. N. Junction

Diode
Symbol

Cathode Negative
N Material

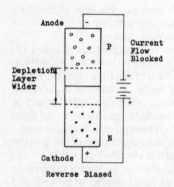

Anode

Current
Flow
Blocked

Depletion
Layer
Wider

Cathode

Reverse Biased

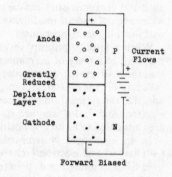

Anode

Current
Flows

Greatly
Reduced
Depletion
Layer

Cathode

Forward Biased

Fig. 127(a) Reverse Bias

Fig. 127(b) Forward Bias

When the connections to the terminals of the supply are reversed so that the P material is connected to the positive terminal and the N material to the negative terminal, holes are driven away from the positive terminal into the depletion or barrier region as are the electrons from the negative terminal. Carriers are present immediately at the junction and across it so that there is a low resistance to any current flow. In this case the condition of the junction is said to be *forward biased* (Fig. 127(b)).

A rectifier is a device which converts an alternating current into a unidirectional current either by the inversion or the suppression of alternate half waves. The two pieces of doped semi-conductor material have this capability and the arrangement is called a pn *Junction Rectifier*, and as it contains only an anode (+ charges) and a cathode (– charges) it is called also a *diode*, with the symbolic representation as in Fig. 126.

Rectification is one of the most important applications of such diodes. Remembering that by altering the polarity of the supply terminals, a current

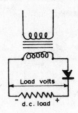

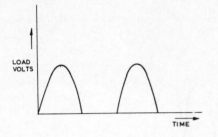

Fig. 128(a) Half-Wave Rectification

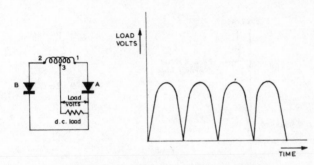

Fig. 128(b) and (c) overleaf   Full-Wave Rectification

could be made to flow or be stopped across the PN junction, then if an alternating sinusoidal voltage is applied to the semi-conductor materials, as it moves through the phase where the P material is connected to the positive terminal and the N material to the negative one, a current will flow (forward biased) but in the reverse phase, when the P material is connected to the negative terminal and the N material to the positive (reverse biased) no current will flow. Thus, in the load, current will flow in one direction only, (see Fig. 128(a)). This is known as half-wave rectification.

The use of a second diode enables conduction of electrons in the band throughout the whole cycle to be achieved. If, at the moment under consideration, point 1 is positive with respect to centre tap point 3 and point 2 is negative, the Diode A is conducting as it is forward biased, and current flow is from 1 through A and dc_{load} to the centre tap. One half period later, 2 becomes positive to 3, B is forward based and the current flow is from 2 through B through dc_{load} and back to the centre tape. The voltage is as shown in Fig. 128(b).

A problem associated with the operation of the above is that the transformer secondary circuit has to produce twice the voltage of that used in the halfwave rectifying circuit, as only half of the winding is in use at any one time, and to overcome this problem a *Bridge Rectifier* is used when point 1 is positive with respect to 2 diodes A and C conduct. When the polarity between 1 and 2 reverses, diodes B and D conduct. This is then a full wave rectifier (Fig. 128(c)). In the above circuits the voltage is undirectional but it is not a steady or uniform

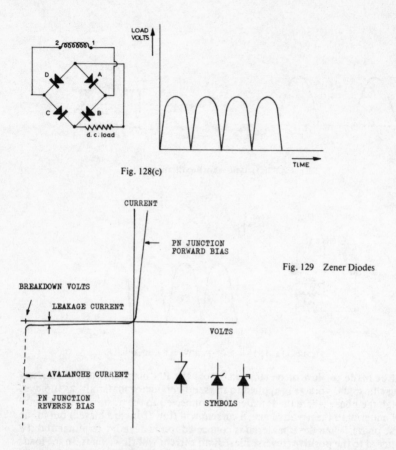

Fig. 128(c)

Fig. 129   Zener Diodes

voltage and therefore filters are used to level the pulses out. These take the form of capacitors, inductors or resistors. Inductors are sometimes known as chokes as they block any current variations and allow the conduction of only d.c. A simple choke is achieved by putting a capacitor in parallel with the load but it has to be large to store a sufficient charge to maintain the current during the time rectifier is not conducting. The procedure is known as filtering or smoothing.

When a PN junction diode is biased in the reversed direction, positive material to negative terminal, etc., the holes at the p-side and electrons on the n-side move away from the junction. The barrier or depletion layer then thickens, the resistance becomes very high and only a small leakage current flows. This leakage current remains small up to a certain voltage value and, once this value has been exceeded, there is a sudden and very large rise in the reverse current. The voltage at which this sudden rise occurs is known as the breakdown voltage. It will not destroy the diode material as long as the power dissipation does not exceed the maximum allowed for the device. Over the operating range of the reverse current, the voltage across the diode remains nearly constant. Such devices are known as *Zener Diodes* (Fig. 129).

Silicon Controlled Rectifiers or **Thyristors** are semi-conductor materials as shown in Fig. 130. Powers of tens of kilowatts can be controlled by these devices, using a small current from a signal source to start the action. They are

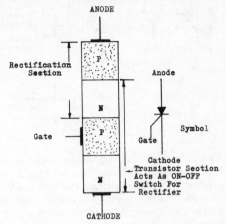

Fig. 130 Thyristor

low voltage, high-current devices which, when in series with a load resistance and a d.c. source, prevent a current flowing in the direction, making the anode negative. When the supply voltage polarity is reversed, making the anode positive, the device is still non-conducting until the gate electrode is made sufficiently positive to provide a gate current exceeding a certain critical value. Once this happens the gate loses control and the current is then determined by the resistance of the external circuit and the value of the anode supply voltage. It can only be shut off by switching off, introducing a very high resistance, or reversing the anode voltage.

Signal amplification can be achieved by using semi-conductor material to form two PN junctions. The configuration can be either pnp or npn with the centre section known as the 'base' controlling the flow of electrons by varying the concentration of charges. Of the other two sections one is known as the *emitter* because it emits electrons, the other the *collector*, as it collects electrons.

Fig. 131 shows the arrangement of an npn transistor or amplifier. The base is usually less than 0·02 mm thick in practice. In the arrangement shown when there are no external applied voltages, the collector and emitter function depletion layers are about the same and will depend upon the amount of doping in collector, emitter and base.

Under normal operating conditions, the circuit is arranged to have the base-emitter junction forward biased so that a current flows easily in the signal or input circuit. The collector-base junction is also arranged to have reverse bias from the main supply voltage and the depletion layer is therefore thick.

With this npn transistor formation, if a small signal which is positive to the emitter is passed into the base, then it causes a number of holes to be injected into the region and in turn the emitter passes an equal number of electrons. Combination does not, however, occur as the base is extremely thin and only lightly doped, and the electron passes into base-collector region and thus into the

135

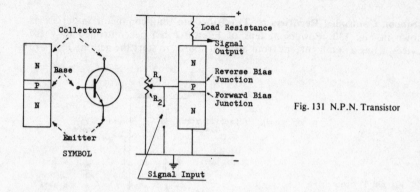

Fig. 131 N.P.N. Transistor

load circuit. In this way many electrons pass into the load circuit before the 'hole' combines with the electron. Thus a small current entering via the base can produce a large load current and so a weak signal from a transducer can be used to produce a strong signal to transmission or control purposes with the strength of the signal controlling the number of, or modulating, the flow of electrons from the emitter into the base.

It must be realized that a bias current to the base in addition to the actual signal value is required, so that any variation in the signal value within certain limits will not cut off the transistor.

An analogy may be drawn with the nozzle/flapper system in which the flapper has to be placed a certain distance from the nozzle to allow an output signal to be produced representing both rises and falls in the condition of the process being monitored. If it was at one extreme for the required process condition, only variations in one direction would be monitored.

The nozzle/flapper gap and consequent air flow for the required operating condition of the process is monitored in the pneumatic equivalent of the bias current. A PNP transistor has a similar mode of operation except that electrons are injected into the base and holes flow from the emitter into the base and thence into the collector (Fig. 132).

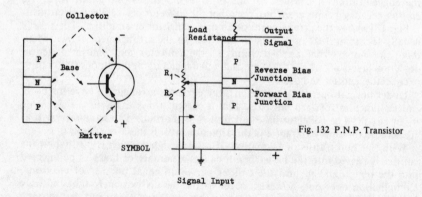

Fig. 132 P.N.P. Transistor

The emitter is designated by having an arrow and the direction of the arrowhead decides whether the transistor is of pnp or npn form. The arrowhead connection is similar to that used for rectifiers and gives the forward current or 'easy' direction of conventional current flow. In Fig. 131 it will be seen that the emitter connection is common to both the signal circuit and the load circuit. This is given the name 'common emitter mode' or 'grounded emitter mode' (as the emitter is connected to earth). This is the most common form for voltage amplification as a small current is drawn from the signal source and enables high voltage gains to be achieved.

To obtain a voltage output from the common emitter amplifier, a load resistor R_{load} is placed between the collector and the supply voltage. The incoming signal will vary the base current, and the varying collector currents will thus produce varying voltages across the load resistor and, as the supply voltage is fixed, this means that the collector voltage must vary. As the base voltage increases in an npn transistor, so the base current increases, and also the collector current. The volt drop across R_{load} increases and the voltage on the collector falls. From this it can be seen that rises of input voltage are accompanied by falls in output voltage and the two voltages are thus 180° out of phase. With a pnp the effect is similar. The voltage in Fig. 132 across the outer lines is maintained constant by a battery or other power supply. By adjusting the resistances R_1 and R_2 the base can be maintained at a steady bias to give the required operating condition. The use of capacitors ensures the elimination of any stray d.c. components with a.c. amplifiers. When the current flowing in the output is so great that it becomes insensitive to changes in the input, the transistor is said to be *saturated*.

Zener Diodes are a particular application of a PN junction which is reversed biased. When this happens the barrier of depletion layer becomes thicker and a very high resistance occurs. There is a leakage current which is very small for all reverse voltages up to a certain value. When this value is exceeded, a very large rise in the reverse current occurs and the voltage at which this happens is known as the breakdown voltage, but is non-destructive within power dissipation limits. Within the operating range of reverse current it is found that the voltage across the diode remains nearly constant and this makes these devices particularly suitable for voltage reference elements, over voltage protection, voltage limiter and biasing, etc. (see Fig. 129).

A **Field Effect Transistor** employs a simple p- or n-type semi-conductor crystal with a 'source' terminal at one end and a 'drain' terminal at the other, carriers passing from source to drain pass through a channel between n- or p-type layers, called the 'gate'. By reverse biasing these layers the barrier layer effect can be altered and thus the width of the channel or gate adjusted to control the flow of carriers. By changing the input signal, therefore, the resistance of the semi-conductor material can be altered controlling the current between source and drain (Fig. 133).

An **Integrated Circuit** is commonly used in electronic work and this consists of a single crystal of silicon, usually 'p' type, in which slices of 'n' type and 'p' type are fixed and covering them with an insulating oxide layer. The connecting metallic conductors are impressed on this. A basic two transistor circuit is shown in Fig. 134 but entire systems such as counters and memories for digital equipment and complex amplifier circuits can be involved.

When using semi-conductor materials it must be remembered that temperature

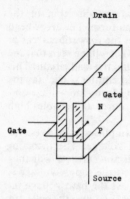

Fig. 133 Field Effect Transistor

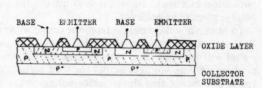

Fig. 134 Integrated Circuit

is an important factor and high temperatures can lead to leakage currents which, if not properly controlled, can lead to unsatisfactory transistor operation and possibly irreparable damage. Germanium transistors have lower operating temperatures than silicon.

An **Operational Amplifier** is a device which can operate on input voltages in a manner similar to those operations carried out by a mathematician. By suitable arrangement of feedback and input impedances, such a device can add, subtract, differentiate, and integrate voltages applied to the input terminals.

The sensing devices described in the text of the previous chapters may be divided overall into two basic types, **Digital** and **Analogue**. By digital representation of a quantity, is implied a number which increases or decreases in steps as increments (or small changes) in the condition of the process being monitored occur. A car milometer indicates the distance travelled in steps of miles and tenths of a mile—this is a form of digital representation. Analogue representation is typified by the traditional steam pressure gauge, where the measured quantity is converted into the pointer position on a circular scale and the pointer position is said to be the analogue of the steam pressure in the boiler.

Bourdon tubes, bi-metallic strips, and filled system devices with mercury or gas filled capillary tubes and bulbs, and mechanical devices may be used to operate a series of electrical contacts in steps to produce a digital signal.

These devices may also be used to produce analogue signals for remote reading by replacing the stepped electrical contacts with a variable resistance or wiper arm, but vibration may cause the arm to bounce on the resistance wire, and over a period of time, dirt, oil and grease as well as wear and corrosion due to dampness may cause the wire to give a false reading or break.

Thermistors, strain gauges, variable capacitors, inductors and transformers, as with as bourdon tubes, bi-metallic strips and capillary bulbs can be constructed to withstand the extremes of temperature, vibration and humidity frequently found in the marine environment, and are frequently used for remote alarm, logging and control applications despite the more complex electric circuitry and increased cost, particularly with regard to the former.

With regard to actuators, electric types are coming more into use as they are positive in action and fail safe 'as is' on power failure, but they can be slow, heavy for the power they produce and can require considerably increased maintenance compared with pneumatic and hydraulic types. They can also present serious problems if required to be used in hazardous areas.

Pneumatic actuators are considerably cheaper, and may be smaller and lighter for large powers, depending upon the air pressures used, but with an electrical control system the provision of a separate air circuit and an electro-pneumatic signal converter is an added expense. The compressibility of air tends to make them slower. They can give fail safe 'as is' or return to one extremity.

Hydraulic actuators have a fast positive response, they can be very powerful for a small size and weight and fail safe 'as is', or return to either extremity by using a lock-in valve. (This is a small spring loaded valve with hydraulic pressure holding it open by means of a piston opposing the spring. If the pressure fails, the spring closes the valve, trapping the oil pressure in the hydraulic cylinder and holding the piston in its last position). A digital signal by means of a solenoid valve can give smooth stepless movement. The main drawback is high oil pressure in the control system and variation in oil viscosity produced by changes in ambient temperature, as well as the cost of filters, pumps and regulators.

WARNING

The following is of particular interest to those concerned with electronic equipment on board ships and is an extract from a Department of Trade Merchant Shipping Notice No. M646. This notice draws attention to a possible health hazard from Beryllium Oxide (Beryllia) material, the dust of which is toxic. The material is used in certain components employed in electronic equipment such as power transistors, particularly VHF types, power diodes, thyristors, ceramic material, where identified by blue colouration or black lines and heat sink washers (highly polished and of dark brass appearance). Some makes of cathode ray tubes are coated on the inside with a ceramic beryllium oxide mixture.

Beryllia is highly dangerous in a dust form when it might be inhaled or enter a cut or skin irritation area. If dust is caused as a result of chafing, filing or breakage and if inhaled, a single exposure lasting minutes or seconds can cause injury to skin or mucous membranes severe enough to endanger life or cause permanent injury. Particles penetrating the skin through wounds or abrasions are liable to cause chronic ulcerations. Symptoms of poisoning are indicated by respiratory troubles or cyanosis (grey/blue discolouration of the skin) which may develop within a week or after a latent period extending to several years.

It is preferable to handle Beryllia parts with gloves, tweezers or similar protection, and if it enters the skin it should be dealt with immediately by washing and normal first aid.

It is recommended that no filing, abrading, dipping, machining or excessive heating should be permitted and care taken that parts do not scrape on a rough surface or come into contact with other parts made from Beryllia.

Recommended Reading

Code of Procedure for Marine Instrumentation and Control Equipment, **British Ship Research Association**

Centralized & Automatic Control in Ships, **D. Gray**, *Pergamon Press*

Fundamentals of Marine Control Engineering, **P. T. C. Wilkinson**, *Whitehall Technical Press*

Automation in Merchant Ships, **J. A. Hind**, *Fishing News (Books) Ltd.*

Process Instruments & Controls Handbook, **D. M. Considine**, *McGraw-Hill Book Co., Inc.*

Application of Automatic Machinery & Alarm Equipment in Ships, **B. G. Smith**, *The Institute of Marine Engineers*

Instrumentation & Control Systems, **L. Jackson**, *Thomas Reed Publications Ltd.*

Control Systems for Technicians, **G. T. Bryan**, *The English University Press*

Electronics, **G. H. Olsen**, *Butterworths*

Control Systems for Turbines and Boilers, **D. M. Lindsley** & **T. A. Machell** *Trans. Institute of Marine Engineers*

The Measurement of Vibration as a Diagnostic Tool, **T. Carmody**, *Trans. Institute of Marine Engineers*

Remote Control of Marine Diesel Engines, **F. R. Norris**, *Marine Engineers Review. Marine Media Management*

Modern Techniques in the Control of Ship Machinery, Ships Gear, *Fishing News (Books) Ltd.*

Index